GOING BUST?

How to Resist Bankruptcy and Winding Up

GOING BUST?

How to Resist Bankruptcy and Winding Up

By

PROFESSOR MUIR HUNTER,
Q.C., LL.D.(Hon)

Foreword by
Desmond Flynn, Inspector General, The Insolvency Service

TO
GILLIAN PETRIE HUNTER
who first conceived this project

ACKNOWLEDGEMENTS

I owe special thanks to District Judge ALAN SIMONS, of Swindon County Court, for checking my procedures, to HANNAH THORNLEY, Barrister, of Michael Crystal QC's Chambers, 3/4 South Square, Gray's Inn, for her invaluable research, to DANIEL KILLINGLEY of the Legal Services Commission, to LISA COLCLOUGH, National Money Advice Policy and Development Officer, Citizens Advice, to STEVE HYNES, Chairman, Law Centres Federation, and to MARY MUIR, of Shaftesbury, Dorset for putting the whole book on Microsoft Word.

DISCLAIMER OF LIABILITY

This book is intended to help those who read it with their efforts, as "litigants in person", to defend their interests, or to assert their rights, in a situation of, or the likelihood of, bankruptcy or winding-up, without the assistance of legal advice or legal representation in court.

Attempts have been made to translate legal terms used in court and in legal documents into the language of everyday speech, and to explain the court procedures as clearly as possible.

However, this work is not a substitute for legal advice in relation to any particular case. Although the author has attempted to produce a work which is designed to assist litigants in person, he does not undertake any duty of care to any person or entity whatsoever, without limitation, in relation to any of the statements in, or omissions from, this work, and accepts no legal liability or responsibility in respect of any statements in or omissions from this work.

MUIR HUNTER

CONTENTS

FOREWORD

My experience of working in the Official Receivers' offices in London and Birmingham was that individuals going bankrupt, almost without exception, had little or no understanding of the process of bankruptcy, or what it meant for them as they tried to sort out and get on with their lives. This was true even if, in many other areas, they were highly qualified or experienced.

Those of us who think we understand the complexities of personal insolvency will almost certainly have relied upon successive editions of *Muir Hunter on Personal Insolvency*, a long-standing and definitive guide to professional understanding. For most people a detailed knowledge of insolvency is not high on the list of their priorities although, sadly, an increasing number are finding themselves in severe financial difficulties. For anyone facing such difficulties, for those advising them or for the general reader Professor Muir Hunter's book offers concise and practical guidance through the labyrinth that is personal bankruptcy. In doing so it sets out the legal principles involved with great clarity and gives clear meaning to a host of difficult legal expressions.

This handbook is the product of enormous learning and experience. I congratulate Professor Muir Hunter on distilling the subject into such clear and comprehensible form.

Desmond Flynn
Inspector General
The Insolvency Service

PREFACE

YOU DON'T HAVE TO GO BANKRUPT OR BE WOUND UP - BUT IF YOU DO, HERE'S HOW TO COPE WITH IT

Who this book is for, and what it is about.

For people in business

You are a small businessman or businesswoman, running a small business or a professional practice or service, or some other occupation.

You run it either personally, or as a partnership, or through a small family company, made up of yourself, your husband, wife, partner, or civil partner, perhaps including the children or some relations. You or the family have financed the business, the partnership or the company by giving guarantees to banks or suppliers, or by mortgaging your home or other homes. You are worried about your debts. You fear you cannot pay them, or the company or the partnership cannot pay them. What will happen to you then? What will happen to the family's homes?

You fear you may be made bankrupt. Or you fear your company or your partnership may be made bankrupt, that is, wound-up or liquidated.

You, or the company or your partnership, may have already received summonses or legal papers about your debts or its debts. You don't know where to turn.

For the person not in business, but owing a lot of money

You may not be in business yourself, you may not work through a company or a partnership. You may instead be employed at a salary, or on piecework, or freelance, or for a weekly or monthly wages-packet.

Life has become very expensive; you may have had unusual expenditures, such as on medical operations off the NHS, or with the children's schools, or with periods of unemployment or not earning. So your debts have mounted up.

You owe a lot of money on your credit cards, and you may be in arrears with payments on the house or the flat, to the bank or the building society.

You are worried how to cope with all the people and firms you owe money to. You keep reading about all the people who are going bankrupt, either by being made bankrupt by their creditors, or making themselves bankrupt.

What should you do for yourself, or let your creditors do to you?

This is not a book on debt-management, or financial down-sizing, or how to make a pint pot spread to a quart. It is to help you to defend, so far as possible, your status and your way of life, to do what can be done, what may be usefully done, in coping with the situation created by a host of impatient creditors, and too few assets.

The first set of Parts of the book, Chapters 3 to 25, deals with the problem of personal bankruptcy, whether of a person in business or not in business - what are the procedures, the dangers and the consequences. The second set of Parts of the book, Chapters 26 – 42, deals with the problems of the winding-up of your company or your partnership.

Lawyers are expensive, even for a first visit to get some advice. You have heard that legal aid is difficult to get, and may not even be available for business people like you.

What you need is a D I Y Handbook, to put you in the picture, mark out the paths, warn of the dangers. Explain the legal mumbo-jumbo. What you can do, and what you can't do.

This is such a book.

This book will help you to protect yourself, your wife, husband, partner, family, to protect your home, your assets, your company's assets, or your partnership's, to protect your future and theirs.

This book will help you to defend yourself and them, in or out of court.

Muir Hunter

PART I
INTRODUCTION

CHAPTER 1
DEFINITIONS

WHAT IS BANKRUPTCY? WHAT IS WINDING UP?

Bankruptcy is what happens to you when the Bankruptcy Court makes a bankruptcy order against you. Inside Greater London this would be the High Court; outside Greater London it would be your local county court. This will come about as the result of a legal application (called "a bankruptcy petition"), made to the court by one of your unpaid creditors, to whom you owe a sum of £750 or more.

The effect of the making of a bankruptcy order against you is to take away the ownership and control of practically all your property, and to put it into the hands of a public official. This official will be either "the Official Receiver" (who works for the Department of Trade and Industry), or the "Trustee in Bankruptcy", who is an accountant or lawyer who specialises in managing the property of bankrupts.

Bankruptcy procedure is explained in Parts I to V, Chapters 3 – 25.

WHAT IS WINDING-UP?

Winding-up, or liquidation, is the process by which a limited company or a partnership is made bankrupt. This will come about as a result of an application (called "a winding-up petition") made to the bankruptcy court (called, in the case of companies and partnerships, the Companies Court or the Winding-Up Court) by one of the company's or the partnership's unpaid creditors, to whom it owes a sum greater than £750. The effect of a winding-up order, made in the Winding-up Court, is to take away nearly all the powers of the directors over the company's property, and of the partners over the partnership property. The control of their property then passes into the hands either of the Official Receiver (see above), or of a public official called "the liquidator", an accountant or lawyer like the trustee in bankruptcy.

The winding-up procedure applies generally to partnerships, though with some differences, described in Chapter 27.

Winding-up proceedings are explained in Parts VI and VIII below, Chapters 26 – 42.

WHAT HAPPENS AFTER THE MAKING OF A BANKRUPTCY OR A WINDING-UP ORDER?

The property of a bankrupt person, and of a wound-up company or partnership, after paying costs and expenses, is sold and divided up among their or its creditors, according to what each creditor is entitled to.

If you become bankrupt, or your company or partnership is wound up, you, or you and its other directors, or its partners, have to hand over all your or its business papers, books, cash, etc., to the Official Receiver, or to the trustee in bankruptcy, or to the liquidator, as you are required to do. You must also answer, on oath, as a bankrupt or as a director or member of a wound-up company or partnership, any questions any one of them puts to you about the working or details of your business or of the company's business. All these matters are dealt with in detail in separate chapters of the book.

The law explained in this book is the law applying to England and Wales. The law of bankruptcy is different in Scotland, in the Channel Islands and (in some respects) in Northern Ireland and the Isle of Man.

CHAPTER 2
A BRIEF HISTORY OF BANKRUPTCY

The first laws on bankruptcy were passed in the time of King Henry VIII, in the 16th century. English merchants had started big export-import businesses, and were running up debts they could not pay, or losing their merchant ships through wars, or blockades, or storms. Shakespeare's play, *The Merchant Of Venice*, is about one such merchant, who believes his ships have been lost at sea, so he cannot pay his creditor, Shylock. Merchants who ran out of money often fled abroad to foreign countries, where the English law could not reach them; such running-away became a serious offence in itself.

So the first bankruptcy laws were very severe; bankrupts could be sent to prison, put in the stocks, or even executed. Over the last five hundred years, the bankruptcy laws have varied in their toughness, but have remained pretty ruthless, until the present Government started reforming them.

Under the Blair Government's new laws, the bankruptcy law, and the laws relating to the winding-up of insolvent companies, have become milder. The Government has a policy called "Rescue Culture"; the idea is, that people and companies should not be made bankrupt or wound-up, if their businesses have value, and can be "rescued" and reconstructed, so as to be able to trade again. One of the Government's books about these proposals was called *Bankruptcy: A Second Chance*.

It is not all jam, however; there is also the medicine. People, companies and partnerships, who go bust in a respectable way, who stop trading when they can see that they are running out of cash, and who treat their creditors fairly and honestly, are to be treated well, and the bankrupts are to be quickly discharged. But those bankrupts and company directors and partners who behave wrongly, recklessly or dishonestly, are to be severely penalised, and may be disqualified from business life for up to fifteen years.

CHAPTER 3

THE LAW OF BANKRUPTCY: LEGAL AID : LITIGANTS IN PERSON

The laws which lay down bankruptcy are to be found in several Acts of Parliament (which will be referred to as "the statutes"). They have many times been amended, that is, altered, added to, corrected or cancelled. So you will hear them referred to as "the Act as amended". The present statutes, dealing with bankruptcies since 1986, are as follows:

- Insolvency Act 1986 (as amended);
- Insolvency Act 2000;
- Enterprise Act 2002, Part 10.

See also Chapter 43, page 179 below.

The statutes usually set out the general pattern of the law; the detail is then filled in by many rules, regulations and orders, (which will be referred to generally as "the rules"). These spell out what sort of procedure is to be used, in each kind of case, and at each stage of it. They also include the official bankruptcy Forms (and for companies the company Forms); in bankruptcy and winding-up cases, wherever court documents have to be used, they have to be written in the way (if any) set out in the official Form for that kind of document. The necessary Forms will be mentioned where necessary.

Copies of some of the necessary Forms are included in the Appendix at pages 186-216, below, for you to copy if you wish, and use for your case. There are Government websites dealing with bankruptcy, where the rules can be read and downloaded; the addresses of those websites are given in the Appendix, at page 206, below.

WHERE TO READ THE LAW, IF YOU REALLY WANT TO

This is not a legal textbook, so it refers in only a few places to any actual sections of the statutes or rules. If you wish to get hold of the statutes and the rules to read for yourself, you should be able to find them in a really big local library, or (more likely) at a Law Centre, or (less likely) at a Citizen's Advice Bureau. Many are available on Government websites.

POSSIBLE LAW BOOKS TO READ

If you really want to read it all up for yourself, my own book *Muir Hunter On Personal Insolvency* (published by Sweet & Maxwell) is regarded as one of the major law books on bankruptcy. I don't edit it any longer; I'm only a consultant editor now. It is updated twice a year, so it's never far behind the latest cases or alterations of statutes or rules. The county court would almost certainly have a copy, and the court staff might allow you to read it. When you are issuing legal proceedings in your case, and you have to go to the court office, you could ask to see the book or other books they may have. The court staff have a duty to help "litigants in person", that is, people involved in cases who can't afford a lawyer to represent them: see below.

There are of course many other books about bankruptcy law, large and small.

LEGAL AID AND ADVICE

Although this book is aimed at you, as a debtor possibly intending to appear in court as a "litigant in person" (see below), you may want, or be obliged, to get legal advice or legal aid to defend yourself, or to claim your rights from one of the organisations, public or charitable, which can provide it. The details of these organisations, and how and where you can apply to them, are set out in Chapter 25, at page 120, below. Legal aid is however difficult, sometimes impossible, to obtain.

LITIGANTS IN PERSON

Everyone who is engaged in a legal proceeding taking place in court has the right to appear in court "in person", and to carry on his case without using a lawyer. He is then called a "litigant in person". He may have with him another person, to advise him, who is called "a lay adviser". That person however cannot address the court on your behalf, except by special permission of the judge, not often given.

There are special rules concerning litigants in person, stating what their rights and duties are, and what legal and court costs they can claim if they win their case: see Chapter 11, p. 41, below). Being a litigant in person is of course not an easy task, but the judge has a duty to help you. If you have been able to study this book, and therefore know something of how things have to be done (or what mustn't be done), I am sure the judge will be grateful: (see Chapters 7 – 14, below, for court procedure).

COMPANIES APPEARING IN COURT "IN PERSON"

For the conditions for a company to appear "in person", without a lawyer, see Chapter 31, page 145 below.

CHAPTER 4
WHAT CAN HAPPEN TO YOU IF YOU DO NOT PAY YOUR DEBTS

A person to whom you owe money is your creditor and you are "the debtor". If you do not pay him, when the money is due, he can take various legal steps against you, to make you pay, or to get the money out of your property. He can take proceedings against you in court, and get a judgment against you, ordering you to pay the money and costs, which is a legal order on you to pay or take the consequences; interest is chargeable on the amount of the judgment, until paid.

But he does not need a judgment for some of the things he can do to you. There are several ways, other than bankruptcy, in which he can try to get payment. They may perhaps be tried on you, so you should know what they are.

Execution: When the creditor has a judgment against you, he can ask the court to order an "execution" of the judgment. This is done by the court ordering its officials – the Enforcement Officers in the High Court, and the Bailiffs in the county court – to enter your home or your business premises (by force, if necessary), and seize whatever of your goods or other property they find there, up to a value they estimate is likely to be enough to meet the amount of the judgment and costs, and their own charges (which can be quite high). The goods and property they seize will be kept for a time, and then sold by auction, often at rather low prices, unless redeemed by the "execution debtor" or his family or friends.

A Third Party Debt Order: Your creditor can apply to the court for an order, called "a third party debt order", to seize money that is owed to you by some one else, such as your credit balance at your bank or building society, or money otherwise owed to you and payable, such as the price of goods which you have sold. This used to be called "a garnishee order". The proceeds, after costs and expenses are met, go towards paying the judgment debt.

A Charging Order: Your creditor can apply to the court for a charging order, which is an order, rather like a mortgage, which can be made against any house property or land which you may own, or your shares or other securities, or interests under a trust, under which he can eventually get a sale, with the net proceeds going to pay the judgment debt.

Distress for Unpaid Rent: This can be done by your landlord, putting bailiffs into your home to seize and sell your furniture.

Bankruptcy: This is the commonest way for your creditors to try to get paid by you or out of your assets. They may apply singly, or several acting together, perhaps needed to make up the minimum sum of £750 required for a bankruptcy application. This is the way with which this book hopes to help you to deal.

CREDIT AGENCIES AND REGISTRATION OF CREDIT DEFAULTERS

If you do not pay your debts, you are very likely to end up having your name registered on the files of credit agencies, where people who deal with you, and your creditors, can look up your credit history. They also register bankruptcies, company liquidations, and the names of people or companies who enter into the kinds of debt agreement called "voluntary arrangements" (referred to in Chapters 24 and 41, pages 107 and 175 below). Once you are on their registers, it may be difficult to get bank or building society credit, or the renewal of credit cards or the issue of new ones.

If you have been made bankrupt and have obtained your discharge or you get an annulment, you can get a certificate from the court of your discharge (which will cost you £60), with which you can apply to the credit agencies to remove the entry of your bankruptcy. You will receive a copy of the order of annulment. You can ask the Secretary of State to put an advertisement of your annulment in a newspaper, at no cost to yourself.

WHAT DEBTS CANNOT BE CLAIMED THROUGH BANKRUPTCY PROCEEDINGS

Certain debts cannot be claimed against you by means of proceedings in bankruptcy, and creditors for those debts cannot claim to share in your property in bankruptcy. These excepted debts are listed in Chapter 22, at p.95, below.

An important change has recently taken place with the making of new rules. If you have been made bankrupt on or after 1st April 2005, payment of lump sum orders made in family proceedings, and orders for the payment of the costs of those proceedings, can now be claimed as debts due to be paid in bankruptcy.

Alternative Procedures

There are alternative legal procedures, which can be applied for by persons or companies unable to pay their debts, to avoid them being made bankrupt or wound-up; see Chapter 24, page 107, below.

Proposed New Procedures

More alternative procedures are being prepared by the Government in late 2006 for the assistance and protection of persons unable to pay their debts, in a Bill now before Parliament; see Chapter 43, page 179 below.

CHAPTER 5
WHO CAN BE MADE BANKRUPT?

This book refers to the bankrupt as "he"; but this should be read as including "she". In bankruptcy women and men are equal.

The creditor's statement that you owe the debt claimed in the statutory demand and in the petition does not, just by itself, make you liable to be made bankrupt on that claim. You must be a person capable of being made bankrupt under the law.

The conditions, at least one of which must apply to you for you to be made bankrupt, are as follows:

(1) You were "domiciled" in England and Wales on the day when the petition was presented to the court and issued. "Domiciled" means that your permanent residence is in England and Wales; but your domicile can be changed, by your moving to other countries, as a permanent change of residence. You may be legally resident in this country, so as to make you domiciled here, even though your residence is illegal, e.g. as an illegal immigrant, or a failed asylum-seeker.
   or
(2) You were personally present in England and Wales on the day when the petition was presented to the court and issued:
   or
(3) You had been "originally resident", or had had a place of residence, in England and Wales, at any time during the three years before the petition was presented to the court and issued:
   or
(4) During those three years, you carried on business in England and Wales, personally or through an agent or manager. The court can decide that you are still "carrying on business" in this country, even though you closed the business down, if you have gone

abroad, leaving business debts of that business (including taxes) still owing and unpaid.

If you wish to apply to set aside the statutory demand, or to dispute the petition, because none of these conditions apply to you, you must assemble quickly all the evidence available to show that, especially documents, passports, purchase deeds of foreign residences, government certificates of foreign residences, licences to carry on business in foreign countries, foreign registrations of marriages or births, etc.

WHO CANNOT BE MADE BANKRUPT?

Children cannot be made bankrupt, except on a claim for the price of things they agreed to buy and which are "necessary" for them to have. Persons employed by a foreign embassy or consulate, or by the United Nations, or by the European Union, or some other international organisations, may also be protected from being made bankrupt. A mentally unfit person may, in some cases, not be made bankrupt.

CHAPTER 6
BEING MADE BANKRUPT; MAKING YOURSELF BANKRUPT

A. BY YOUR CREDITOR

If your creditor decides to try to obtain payment of his debt by making you bankrupt, he may issue a **statutory demand** for the debt, or debts, which he claims that you owe him. If you don't pay the statutory demand within the 21 days allowed for payment, or don't successfully challenge it by applying to set it aside, he can then "present", (that is, issue), and "serve you", (that is, deliver to you), with a legal court document called a **bankruptcy petition**.

In some cases, your creditor can issue a petition against you, without first issuing a statutory demand.

The case is heard in court by a Registrar in the High Court, and by a District Judge in the county court. If the court finds the case against you proved, that you owe the debt, and are insolvent, that is, that you cannot pay your debts as they fall due, it will make a **bankruptcy order,** as a result of which you become a bankrupt.

These legal processes are described and explained in the following chapters.

B. MAKING YOURSELF BANKRUPT

If you are being much harassed by creditors and their executions, and you yourself fit into one of the above conditions, you can get rid of those harassments by making yourself bankrupt, that is, by presenting your own "debtor's petition". Whether it would be wise for you to do so is a matter on which you really ought to get some legal advice; a bankruptcy order always has serious consequences for the bankrupt.

There are two difficulties here. First, you will have to pay a court fee of £190, and a deposit of £370; secondly, you will have to complete a long and detailed **statement of affairs**. This is a lot more complicated than the sort of statement which you have to make, when you are made bankrupt by a creditor. You also have to state that you cannot pay your debts as they fall due. You may be able to be let off the court fee, on application to the court, but you cannot be let off the deposit.

You have to go to the local court which can make you bankrupt, to collect the forms for the petition and for the statement of affairs. This will be the court which hears bankruptcy cases, over the area in which you live or carry on your business. This court will be:

(1) If you live within "the London insolvency district" (roughly, Greater London, including the City of London), you will apply to the High Court, in the Strand, London. This is the bankruptcy court for everyone who lives or works within the court areas of the following county courts: Barnet, Bloomsbury, Bow, Brentford, Central London, Clerkenwell, Edmonton, Lambeth, Mayor's & City of London, Shoreditch, Wandsworth, West London, and Willesden.

(2) Everyone outside that area must go to their local county court, if it does bankruptcy cases, if not, to the nearest county court which does. To get information about these things, ring up your nearest county court, and they will tell you, or you can consult the Court's web site on the internet.

PAPERS FOR THE COURT

If you decide to present your own petition, you will need to complete Form 6.27, and the form for the statement of affairs (Form 6.28). Form 6.27 is included in the Appendix at page 190, but not Form 6.28, which is supplied by the court. For presenting the petition, you will need to prepare the original petition and three copies, and the original of the statement of affairs (on which you must swear an affidavit - see Chapter 9, page 31, below), and two copies, so this will take a good deal of time, effort and money to carry out. To be sure of getting it all right, you will probably need help which you will find the court officials very ready to give you.

If your total debts are below £40,000, and your property is worth more than £4,000, the court may perhaps decide not to make a bankruptcy order against you, but may appoint "an insolvency practitioner", (that is, a bankruptcy specialist), to report on the possibility of making a voluntary arrangement with your creditors, which would avoid bankruptcy (see Chapter 24, below).

A copy of Form 6.27 is printed in the Appendix at page 190, below.

THE COST TO YOUR CREDITOR OF MAKING YOU BANKRUPT

It may be worth reminding the creditor, if negotiating with him about his debt, or his statutory demand, what it is likely to cost him to get a bankruptcy order against you.

(1) His solicitors must draft the details of the debt and the statutory demand, and serve it on you personally. Solicitors' charges (including service), say, £300.

(2) If you apply to set aside the demand, his solicitors must reply to your case, and must appear, with or without a barrister, if a hearing is ordered. Solicitors' charges, say £500, plus VAT.

(3) If your application is dismissed, his solicitors must draft the petition, and serve it on you personally. The court fee is £190, plus a deposit of £370, plus solicitors' charges, say £350, total £910, plus VAT.

(4) Whether you dispute the petition or not, and even if you don't appear, his solicitors, with or without a barrister, must prepare an affidavit of service, certificate of continuing debt, and list of supporting creditors, and then appear at the hearing of the petition and apply for the bankruptcy order. Solicitors' charges, say £400, plus VAT. If you dispute the petition, at a contested hearing, their charges will increase to, say £900, plus VAT.

Possible outlay, if the statutory demand and the petition are both disputed, £2,210, (plus VAT where shown).

PART II
BANKRUPTCY

CHAPTER 7
BANKRUPTCY USUALLY BEGINS WITH A STATUTORY DEMAND

If you have not paid one of your creditors a debt of £750 or over, and have not replied to his letters demanding payment, he is likely to "serve you with", that is, deliver to you, a legal document called a **statutory demand**, with which most bankruptcies begin. A statutory demand is explained in Chapter 8, below.

When you receive a statutory demand for a debt, which you can't pay or don't want to pay, you should, if possible, see a lawyer about what you can and should do about it. If you can afford a lawyer, you should look for a solicitors' firm which states that it handles bankruptcy cases, and whether they are licensed to do legal aid work (now re-named "community funded legal service"). Whether you can get legal aid depends on what your means are in income and capital, and whether you have a good case. But, as you are threatened with bankruptcy, you ought to try to get a session with them under the "Legal Help" scheme. See Chapter 25, at page 117, below, and the Appendix at page 183, below, for details of legal aid and assistance, and the organisations which can provide it.

There are fewer solicitors' firms doing legal aid work nowadays, so you may not be able to find one working near enough to where you live. You could try to find a Law Centre or you could go to a Citizen's Advice Bureau. The Law Centre might be able to provide you with a lawyer to go into court, but the Citizen's Advice Bureau is not very likely to be able to provide you with one.

If you are left with no one to give you legal help to fight the statutory demand, this book is here to try to fill the gap. Its job is to help you to understand the case against you, and to make such defence to it as the facts and the law can provide you with. It is also here to help you to carry out the necessary legal steps in the way of procedures, forms and court rules. This should keep you on the right path with the court, and help you to present your case as well as possible.

The book also describes the consequences to you and your family of your being made bankrupt, and what the effect is on your earnings, home, etc., and what your rights are, as a bankrupt.

CHAPTER 8
UNDERSTANDING THE STATUTORY DEMAND

The **statutory demand** is issued by your creditor and, in the ordinary way, is "served" on you personally: that is, brought to your home or business address, or possibly given to you in the street, by a person called a "process-server". He will usually try to make an appointment with you for personal service, to which you should agree. It will not do you any good to refuse to accept service; in fact, it may do you harm when it comes to hearing your case.

DON'T TRY TO AVOID SERVICE OF THE STATUTORY DEMAND

Don't try to avoid service, e.g. by leaving home without leaving a forwarding address, or by refusing to open the door to the process-server, or by getting your partner to say you are not at home. If you do, the creditor can get an order to serve the statutory demand on you in other ways: by first-class post, or by putting it through your letter-box, or, in the case of an evasive customer, by inserting an advertisement in the newspaper the debtor usually reads.

If service of legal papers has to be done in any of those ways, it makes for complications for you when counting the number of days within which you must pay up – or take defensive action.

The statutory demand is a long document, running to a number of pages. It can come in one of three official forms, according to whether the debt the creditor claims from you is:

a) an ordinary debt due and payable at once (Form 6.1); or
b) a judgment debt (being a sum of money which a court has or-dered you to pay in other proceedings) (Form 6.2); or

c) a "future debt", payable at a certain future date (Form 6.3), see page 29, below).

The only difference between the three forms of statutory demand is in the description of the debt.

You should now go through the Statutory Demand, Forms 6.1, 6.2, or 6.3, reading the notes below.

Page 1 (all forms)
This gives you the creditor's name and address (or names and addresses if there is more than one creditor); and a statement of the total sum of money claimed.

Page 2: Particulars of Debt
The creditor sets out here the particulars of debt, the date(s) on which he claims the money became owed; what the money claimed is to be paid for (that is, what you received from him); and the total sum due at the date of the demand.

Page 2-3: The Make-up of the Debt: Interest
The total amount claimed may, in addition to the actual debt, include a sum by way of interest. If the debt is a judgment debt, to be paid by order of the court, the creditor has the right to add interest at 8%, from the date of the judgment order.

If the debt is *not* a judgment debt, it will only carry interest in one of three ways:

  (i) if the payment of interest on the sum to be paid was agreed, by word of mouth or in writing, at the time the debt came into being, or afterwards;
 (ii) if the court ordered interest to be added to the sum of money claimed and ordered to be paid; or
(iii) if the debt comes under the Act of Parliament which makes interest, at 8%, payable on debts which have become long overdue for payment and remain unpaid, without a good excuse.

The creditor must also state what other charges or additions he is making to the money claimed.

Security

If the creditor holds any security for the debt you owe him, such as a mortgage or a charge or a lien (which is a pledge) over a piece of your property, he must put an estimated value on it, and deduct that value from the total sum he is claiming from you in his statutory demand.

Such a security is an agreement between you and your creditor, whereby you have given him the right to hold, or to own the legal rights to, that piece of property, until you have paid him the amount (with interest, if agreed) "charged" on it, and the further right, if you do not pay him the full amount due, in accordance with your agreement with him, to sell it.

The creditor's estimated value of his security, when deducted from the total amount he is claiming, **must leave at least £750 due. If it leaves less than that, he cannot proceed against you in bankruptcy,** unless he joins up with another creditor. The value of any security given for your debt by someone else, such as a guarantee of payment, does not have to be deducted from the debt you owe. You can challenge his valuation of his security and say that it is too low.

Page 3: Your right to apply to set the statutory demand aside
You have the right, if you have good reasons for objecting to the creditor's claim, to apply to the court to set aside the statutory demand (see page 29, below). The name and address of the court, to which you will have to make your application, are printed on this page of the statutory demand.

Page 4: Assignment
If the creditor making the statutory demand is not the actual person or company from whom you bought something, or with whom you dealt in incurring the debt, he or it must be claiming the debt as payable to them, as a result of your original creditor having sold ("assigned", as it is called) the debt to them. If this is the case, details of the assignment, that is, the document recording the sale, must be given. You should already have been told of this sale by the substituted creditor.

If the creditor is *not* the person or company with whom you dealt, this may produce problems for them in claiming against you.

Page 5: Payment

Unless you apply to set the statutory demand aside, you have to pay the debt in full as claimed **within 21 days of the date when you received the statutory demand.** You should, therefore, make an immediate note of the date when you received it, usually by personal service (see above). You can apply to the court to extend that period of 21 days, before it has expired and also after it has expired. The court officials will explain how you do this.

What you can do if you don't pay

If you don't want to pay, or cannot pay, within those 21 days, but do not want to be made bankrupt, you must do one of the following things:

a) Write to the creditor (the person named, at the address given in the statutory demand, as the person for you to write to), **offering to give him security for the debt claimed (or more security if he already holds some) for payment within a reasonable time;** or

b) Write to the creditor, **offering to settle or "compound" with him, that is, get him to agree to accept payment by instalments; or a part of the debt, in full and final settlement;** or

c) If you intend to dispute the statutory demand, **make an application to the court to set the statutory demand aside, (see below, Chapter 9). To do this, you must make an application to set it aside within 18 days from the date the statutory demand reached you.** But you can apply to the court to give you more time to do this both before that period has expired and after it has expired: the court official will explain how you do this.

What happens if the creditor does not agree to take security or to compound?

If you do not offer the creditor the security, a settlement or a compounding, as stated above, to which he agrees, or do not apply to set the statutory demand aside, **the creditor can present, (that is, issue), a bankruptcy petition against you, on which the court can make you bankrupt.**

Page 6: Effect of an application to set aside the statutory demand
If you have issued an application to set aside the statutory demand, the creditor cannot issue a bankruptcy petition against you, until after your application has been heard and decided by the court.

When the creditor does not need to issue a statutory demand

If you are liable under a **judgment or order** for the debt claimed by the creditor, and he has tried to collect the debt by some form of **execution**, or **third party debt order** (see above, p. 11), which **either** didn't produce enough money to pay the debt and the extra charges for execution, in full, **or** produced no money at all, then the creditor is entitled to present his petition straightaway **without having to serve you with a statutory demand.**

FUTURE DEBT

The debt of which the creditor claims payment need not be a debt already due and payable. It may be a debt not due and payable till a future date; what the creditor is saying is that when that date arrives, it is not reasonably likely that you will be able to pay it. If this is his case, then the argument will turn on how much, at that date, you will likely be earning or making from your business, job or profession; or how much cash you expect to have available to pay him, at the same time as your other debts then due.

CHAPTER 9
PREPARING THE PAPERS FOR YOUR APPLICATION TO SET ASIDE

To apply to the court to set aside the statutory demand, you will need to complete the legal **application form,** called Form 6.4. There is a copy in the Appendix, page 185 below, or you can get a copy from the court.

To support your application, you will need to put in what is called "written evidence". This is explained at page 32, below; it will be a **Witness Statement,** as there described made by you, with "exhibits": see p. 33, below. The "exhibits" will include a copy of the statutory demand, and any papers or documents which you have about your case. That witness statement must also be made in a legal form, Form 6.5; there is a copy of that in the Appendix at page 187, below, or you can get a copy from the court. It will set out what your objections are to the debt and/or to the statutory demand, on the lines discussed in Chapter 8, above.

PREPARING YOUR WITNESS STATEMENT

Prepare your witness statement with great care, sticking to the facts and events which you know, or can be sure of, having been told by other people whom you should name, or having learned from the papers in the case.

If you are attacking the amount of the creditor's debt, you must make "exhibits" out of all the papers which you have, such as invoices, statements of account, letters of complaint, letters demanding payment, your replies, faxes, e-mails, etc., which support the case you are making, or show that his case is mistaken: for an explanation of "exhibits", see p. 33, below.

EVIDENCE: WITNESS STATEMENTS

Evidence, that is, the statements of witnesses, in bankruptcy proceedings is not usually given by word of mouth of a witness standing up in court, as is the rule on the hearing of most other trials of legal cases. It is principally given in writing in one of two forms, either:

(1) **A Witness Statement**

This is a written statement by the witness, saying what he knows about the case, and referring to any papers or documents which he thinks relate to the case. The papers and documents to which he refers and wishes to rely on, are called "**Exhibits to the Witness Statement**" for the rules about these, see page 33, below.

The witness signs the witness statement, and then makes and signs a further statement, verifying what he has written: *"I believe that the facts stated in this Witness Statement are true"*; this is called "**The Statement of Truth**".

(2) **An Affidavit**

This again is a written statement, made by you or your witness, with exhibits of papers and documents. But in the case of an affidavit, the witness does not make a statement of truth; he takes the statement either to a solicitor who is a "commissioner for oaths" (who will charge a fee), or to a court official who is authorised to take oaths (who will not charge a fee); before one or the other, he will swear an oath as to its truth.

WHAT YOU SHOULD PUT INTO YOUR WITNESS STATEMENT OR AFFIDAVIT

A witness statement (or affidavit) should begin with the full name of the person making it (you, or your witness), the address where they live, and/or (if they are a professional business man or woman) the address of the office where they work, and the position they hold in that office.

Expert Witnesses

If your witness is an expert in some profession or some trade which is important for what you want to prove, or disprove, in your case, they should give their qualifications in that skill or experience. Such witness are called "expert witnesses", and there are special court rules regulating them, and the evidence they give. You have to get the court's permission to call them as witnesses, or to put in their reports.

EXHIBITS TO WITNESS STATEMENTS OR AFFIDAVITS

An "exhibit" is a paper, a document or some other thing or object, which forms part of the facts of your case, or supports your arguments, and which you want the court to see, read, or examine.

An exhibit is an object to help you to prove the facts on which you rely, or to disprove some fact on which the creditor relies, or which may otherwise damage the case he is making against you.

It may be a letter, an invoice, a receipt, a newspaper cutting or a photograph. It may even be an object (which must be enclosed in a labelled bag), such as a damaged or defective car part. It must be relevant, that is, it must relate to what the case is about.

If the exhibit is a legal document, forming part of some other case in which you have been involved with the creditor, the copy you make an exhibit must be an official court copy from the papers in that case.

WHAT YOU AND YOUR WITNESSES SHOULD STATE IN YOUR EVIDENCE

In stating the facts of your case, you and your witnesses must make clear:

(a) what facts you know from your own knowledge, or they know from their own knowledge;
(b) what you know, and similarly what they know, from information received from other persons;
(c) what you believe to be true, and what they believe to be true.

Papers and documents, which are referred to in the witness statement and made exhibits to it, should each be separately bound up, and marked with its exhibit number, and, if it is a bundle, supplied with a list of the contents. Each exhibit or bundle should have a front sheet, giving the name of the case and a statement that it is an exhibit to the witness statement of the witness, giving his name and the exhibit number. There is an example of how to mark the exhibits below, and in the Appendix at page 187, below.

THE DIFFERENCE BETWEEN THE TWO FORMS OF STATEMENT

In the case of a witness statement, verified by a statement of truth, if the witness states things in it which he does not honestly believe to be true, he is liable to be sent to prison by the court for **Contempt of Court**. In the case of an affidavit, if he states things in it which he does not honestly believe to be true, he is liable **to be prosecuted and sent to prison for perjury.**

USE OF WITNESS STATEMENTS

Witness statements may now be used in all bankruptcy cases (and also in winding-up cases), except where affidavits are still specially required.

FORM OF WITNESS STATEMENT

The witness statement should be typed, on A4 paper, double-spaced, and on one side of the paper only; the pages should be securely bound. It should be headed with the name of the case as it appears on the legal documents. On the top right hand corner of the front page, the witness should put the name of the party for whose benefit the statement is being made (that is, yourself), the surname and initials of the witness, the number of the statement or the afffidavit (if the witness has made more than one), the number and marking of any exhibits, and the date of the statement.

A specimen witness statement is printed in the Appendix at page 187, below.

HOW MANY COPIES YOU WILL NEED

To make your application to the court, you have to prepare one original set of papers, and then make **four copies of everything**. One of
these will be your own working copy; the other three have to be
"filed" with the original with the court. You will probably need to
have the copies made at a copy shop; if any of the papers have important things marked on them in colour, have the copies colour-
printed. Remember to keep all the copying and office receipts, as
proof of your expenditure for your costs claim.

If your application is accepted by the court as fit for a hearing with
the creditor, the court will then send completed copies of the application and the other documents to you, to the creditor, and to the
person named in the statutory demand as the person to be written to
about it.

PUTTING THE PAPERS TOGETHER

You have now completed the application form in five copies, and the
same number of copies of your witness statement, and of any witness
statements by any one else whose evidence could help, and for the
exhibits, each properly labelled and bound up.

USING COPIES

Copies of papers and documents can be used as exhibits, provided
that the originals are available to be seen on request by the other side,
and by the court at the hearing. The original exhibits must be filed at
the court with the witness statement to which they belong.

CHAPTER 10
FILING YOUR APPLICATION: THE FIRST HEARING

Now take **the original and three copies** of what you have prepared to the court, to be "filed", that is, handed in and accepted. Make sure that you get there in good time, remembering that they close at 4.00 p.m., and give yourself enough time to do the necessary formalities and paperwork. Tell the court officials that you wish to apply to set aside a statutory demand, and that you have all your papers ready to file.

The court officials will be willing to help you. If they have corrections or suggestions to make about your papers, accept their advice; their advice will probably be right.

When they are satisfied with the papers, they will ask for a fee of £60, and will then put the court's official seal on the application, which gives it legal effect. You can apply to the court to be let off paying this fee, on the grounds of your lack of means.

THE FIRST HEARING OF YOUR APPLICATION

Your completed application will then be put by the court officials before the judge, (that is, in the High Court, the Registrar, in the county court, the District Judge). This will usually not involve you appearing before him yourself; they are for him to read, before the creditor becomes legally involved. If the judge considers that your objections to the statutory demand are not strong enough in law or fact, he will dismiss your application.

If he considers that you have a case, and that your objections could be found to be strong enough, he will fix a place, a date and a time (called "the venue"), where and when you will make your application again, this time at the hearing attended by the creditor, at is described in Chapter 11, page 39 below as "**the Full Hearing**".

The three copies of your application, witness statements, etc. will now be completed by the court with the details of the venue, and will be sent out to give **not less than 7 days' notice of the hearing**, to you, to the creditor, and to the person named in the statutory demand as the person to be written to.

YOU CANNOT OFTEN ARGUE THE SAME POINTS TWICE

This is an important point. Whatever arguments or facts you can bring against the creditor's claim, when applying to set the statutory demand aside, if they are not accepted by the court, you may not be allowed to bring them up again at the next stage of the proceedings, in opposition to the petition; even arguments that you could have used, but did not, may also be barred. So, make the best of every point that you can raise against the statutory demand.

THE CREDITOR'S REPLY AND DEFENCE

When the creditor receives from the court the copies of your application, witness statements, etc., he will reply to what you have put forward in opposition to his statutory demand. He must make his own witness statements, and send copies of them, with his exhibits, to you **not less than 7 days before the hearing**. If, when you receive his evidence, you wish to cross-examine him on what he and his witnesses say, you must apply to the court for an order that they attend the hearing.

WHAT HAPPENS AT THE FIRST HEARING

If the judge does require you to attend before him, he may wish to discuss with you and the creditor what he sees as the issues in the case, and how they should be presented at the Full Hearing.

CHAPTER 11

THE FULL HEARING OF YOUR APPLICATION TO SET ASIDE THE STATUTORY DEMAND

You must appear in court on the day, time and place fixed by the court. You must be very punctual and make sure that you have with you your own copies of all the papers you need for the hearing, and any original documents of which you have only exhibited copies, as well as the court-issued copy of the application. If the creditor has asked you, or the court has directed, that any of your witnesses should attend to be cross-examined, (see below), you must be sure that they are there. If you know that you or they won't be able to be present, for a really good reason, you must write to the court, and to the creditor, as soon as possible in advance of the hearing.

You are entitled to begin. The judge may ask you to briefly explain your case. You may ask him for permission to add new points, which you have later thought of, and want to add to what you and your witnesses have put in the written evidence. He may allow you, in relation to your own evidence, to add to it by word of mouth, and not in writing.

If the judge tells you that he has already read your witness statements or affidavits, you will not need to read them all through again; but you should draw his attention to any specially relevant parts of them, so as to underline their importance to your case.

"CROSS-EXAMINATION"

The creditor, or more probably his lawyer, may wish to cross-examine you or your witnesses. To do this, he must have obtained the court's permission, and he must have given you notice, so as to be sure that your witnesses attend the court.

When he has finished cross-examining you, you can speak again, to restate your view of the case or the facts, which he has been trying to weaken or dismiss. If your witnesses have been cross-examined, you can ask them questions to restore any important parts of their evidence which cross-examination has undermined.

WHAT IS "CROSS-EXAMINATION"?

"Cross-examination" is what the creditor or his lawyer does to you or your witnesses, by asking you or them questions about their witness statements. He does this to try to shake the evidence you or they have given, as to what happened in the case. He wants to make the judge disbelieve them, or treat their evidence as mistaken, or not relevant.

He may ask forceful or upsetting questions. He may suggest that you are, or your witness is, not telling the truth, or are exaggerating what the witness saw, or what he knows, or are mistakenly describing what happened in the case.

Your opponent is allowed to do this, but within certain limits. He may not ask questions which are not relevant to what the case is really about, nor ask questions which are personally offensive to the witness. The court has a duty to protect a witness from being unfairly questioned or bullied. Above all, do not lose your cool, or your temper, and always show great respect to the court, and to your opponents.

DEBT BASED ON A JUDGMENT

If the debt is based on a judgment given after a trial in which you took part, the judge will be most unlikely to allow you to question any of the facts found by the court, on which the judgment is based, in answer to the statutory demand based on it.

If the judge decides against you, he will dismiss your application, probably with costs payable by you. Those costs cannot be added to the debt claimed in the statutory demand. He may "assess", that is, fix, the amount of the costs there and then. For "costs", see below.

OTHER ORDERS THAT CAN BE MADE WHEN YOUR APPLICATION IS DISMISSED

Despite making the order dismissing your application with costs, the court, if it thinks it would be fair to you, may order the creditor not to issue a bankruptcy petition before a certain date, to give you a final chance to settle with him. The court may in addition:

(1) grant you an adjournment of the hearing, that is, postpone the further hearing to a later date, so as to enable you to apply to the court which gave the judgment or made the order against you, to set the judgment or order aside, or
(2) make the order, but grant you a stay, that is, a suspension of the order, while you appeal to a higher court against the order; you will be expected to give some clear indications of your proposed grounds of appeal, that is, in what way you consider the court to have made a wrong decision.

The dismissal of your application to set aside the statutory demand is not the end of your case. The creditor now has to take the next step, which is to draft and "present" (that is, take to the court and issue) a bankruptcy petition, asking for the order to make you bankrupt.

COSTS

Where a party is legally represented

When the court has decided a case, it will almost always make an order that the unsuccessful party shall pay the "costs" of the success-ful party. Sometimes, it will make an immediate "assessment", (that is, the fixing), of the amount of costs; or it may postpone the assess-ment of the amount until a later date, by another judge or official.

The order may be for the payment of the whole of the costs, as as-sessed, or there may be different orders for different parts of the case. A party may have won on some points while losing on others, or may be penalised for mistaken procedures or misconduct of the case. The court makes adjustments for these aspects, reducing the amount awarded, or awarding the unsuccessful party some of the costs.

The party claiming costs has to put in his bill, showing the amounts actually paid out, or due to be paid out by him, or to which he is otherwise entitled, by way of fees for barristers or solicitors, expert and other witnesses, and other expenses, called "disbursements". The court will rarely award the whole of the sums claimed; it either awards what are the fixed "tariff costs" (if there are any), or what are called "party and party costs", fixing a reasonable amount for barristers' and solicitors' fees and disbursements.

The sum fixed by the court for costs becomes part of the judgment, and interest accrues on it until paid.

Where there is a litigant in person

Litigants are entitled to be awarded their costs if successful, though at different rates from those applied where barristers and solicitors are involved; the following rules apply:

(1) A litigant in person is entitled to two-thirds of the amounts which would have been allowed in the case of a legal representative, if the work or expenditure involved had been the same sort as would have been incurred, if done by a legal representative.
(2) He may claim for payments reasonably made for legal services relating to the conduct of the case, including the cost of obtaining expert assistance in assessing his costs claim;
(3) He may claim costs for the time reasonably spent in doing the work for which he is claiming costs, to the extent that he can prove that he suffered financial loss thereby, of which he must produce full details, and serve a copy on the other party.

Otherwise he may claim for his time reasonably spent on the work at the rate of £9.25 per hour. He cannot claim the amount of a witness allowance for himself, as well as claiming under this head.

Companies appearing in person

A company or any other form of corporation, which appears without a legal representative, is a litigant in person for the purpose of these costs rules; see Chapter 31.

CHAPTER 12
THE BANKRUPTCY PETITION

A **bankruptcy petition** is an application to the court by your creditor (now called "the petitioning creditor") for you to be made bankrupt. In the petition, he must state the amount which he is claiming from you as his debt, and any security he holds from you for the debt. He must state that you have not complied with his statutory demand, and that if you have applied to set the statutory demand aside, your application has been dismissed.

The petition will state that you are **insolvent,** that is, that you cannot pay your debts in full when they fall due, and it will ask that a bankruptcy order be made against you.

The petition must be supported by a **witness statement,** made by or on behalf of the petitioning creditor, and verified by a **Statement of Truth:** see, as to these documents, page 31, above. In the witness statement, the petitioning creditor must give his reasons for claiming that you should be made bankrupt.

PETITION BASED ON A JUDGMENT DEBT

Where the debt claimed is based on a judgment or order of a court, ordering you to pay a sum of money, it will be difficult for you to argue that the money is not due. The court which gave the judgment or made the order will be treated as having conclusively decided that it was due, and how much was due.

PETITION FOR A FUTURE DEBT

Where the debt claimed in the petition is a future debt, that is, where the debt, though certain, is not yet due and payable, and will only become due and payable at a later date, the petitioning creditor must give his reasons for believing that when the date for payment arrives, you will not be able to pay it (see page 27, above).

FOR WHOSE BENEFIT IS THE PETITION BROUGHT?

Although the petition is in the name of the petitioning creditor, and claims that you owe him his debt, his claim to a bankruptcy order is made, legally, for the benefit of all your creditors. The court, in deciding to make a bankruptcy order (if it does), and in dealing with your property, must, so far as it can, do what it considers to be right for all your creditors.

It is this rule which makes it difficult sometimes for the person petitioned against to get the petition dismissed by a private deal with the petitioning creditor, because the court may not allow a settlement on such terms.

WHAT THE PETITION MUST STATE

The bankruptcy petition against you must state the following:

Identifying you and your business

(1) The petition must state your full name (so far as known to the creditor), your home address, and what you do by way of a job, occupation or profession;

(2) It must also state:

 (a) the name or names (other than your own), under which you carry on business (if you do), and whether you carry on business alone or with other people;

 (b) the name or names, (other than your own) under which you carried on business, at or after the time when you began to owe the debt to the creditor, and what sort of business it was;

 (c) The nature of your business, and the address or addresses from which you carry it on, or have carried it on;

(d) the place, date and time when you were served with the petition, or, if you were not personally served, how, when and where it was served in another way;

(e) that you have not paid the sum demanded by the statutory demand, and have not made any settlement or compounding with the creditor;

(f) that you have not applied to set the statutory demand aside, or that you have so applied, but your application was dismissed, giving details of the order. While an application by a debtor to set aside a statutory demand is pending before the court, no petition can be issued against him;

(g) the place where, according to the creditor, you have your "centre of main interests";

This is a very technical matter, which has to do with whether, under the bankruptcy laws of the European Union, you also carry on business in other countries belonging to the European Union, where you might also be made bankrupt, and fixing which is the country from which you actually run your business or businesses.

Identifying the debt

The petition must state the amount of the debt claimed, that it is a "liquidated sum" (i.e. a fixed amount), what the money was for, and when it became owed or became due, what (if any) are the charges for interest, and whether there are charges for interest of which you have not previously been told, and any other charges accruing, which have increased the debt.

Petition for a future debt

Where the debt claimed is a *future debt*, the petition must state what the creditor claims to be the fixed time when it will become due and payable.

In the case of such a petition for a future debt, you can apply to the court for an order that the petitioning creditor shall provide security for your costs of the petition.

Petition based on an execution for the debt which did not raise enough money

Where the petition is based not on an unpaid statutory demand, as a basis for saying that you are insolvent, but on an unsuccessful execution over your goods to recover a judgment debt, which yielded no net money, or not enough to reduce the debt below £750, the petition must give details of the execution, and of what the enforcement officers or bailiffs reported as to how much in value (if anything) they had seized.

WHAT YOU HAVE TO DO ABOUT THE PETITION: NOTICE OF DISPUTE

When you have been served with the bankruptcy petition (which can be validly served on you in ways other than personally, if necessary: see Chapter 8, above), it will state the date for hearing, which must not be sooner than 14 days after the date of service.

Notice of Dispute

If you want to oppose the petition, you must, **within seven days before the date fixed for the hearing**, file in court a **"notice of dispute"**, and send a copy to the creditor or his solicitor. If you cannot complete the notice in the time allowed, you can ask the creditor or his solicitor to agree to extend your time, and if they refuse, you can apply to the court.

You should put into the notice what your grounds for disputing are, preferably different or additional grounds to those you raised against the statutory demand. However, although strictly speaking you cannot raise against the petition the same specific grounds of dispute which you raised on the application to set aside the statutory demand, and which were rejected, it may still be worth making a case with them again against the petition, and see if the court will let you.

In drafting your Notice of Dispute, put each point briefly in a separate paragraph.

The scope for settlement

You can also describe what steps (if any) you have taken to try to settle or compound with the creditor. If you have no other creditors, or have settled up with all of them, other than the petitioning creditor, you may propose a settlement with him. If you are able to make an offer to settle with him, which if accepted would lead to the dismissal of the petition, **and the creditor unreasonably refuses it,** the court may refuse to make a bankruptcy order. But this is very difficult to achieve.

The form of the notice of dispute

A Form (Form 6.19) for this is printed in the Appendix, at page 189, below. It will need to be supported by a Statement of Truth (or a witness statement; see Chapter 9, page 31, above).

CHAPTER 13
THE HEARING OF THE PETITION

The petition will be heard by the same court which heard your application (if you made one) to set aside the statutory demand. If the case is in the county court, the District Judge who hears it may possibly not be the same judge who heard your application, but he will have the notes of that hearing. If the case is in the High Court, the Registrar who hears it will usually be the same as the Registrar who heard your application.

The hearing will be again in private. In each court, the judge is to be addressed as "Sir" or "Madam".

You must be very punctual at the hearing, and identify yourself to the court usher. Your case will be listed outside the court where it will be heard. Be sure that you have all the necessary papers. These should include:

- The statutory demand;
- Your witness statement(s) supporting your application, with its exhibits;
- The order made on your application;
- The petition, and the witness statement of the creditor supporting it, with its exhibits and any other witness statements of his other witnesses (if any);
- Your witness statement opposing the petition, with its exhibits;
- Any papers dealing with a possible settlement or "compounding" (i.e. settling for a lower amount) between you and the creditors, UNLESS MARKED "WITHOUT PREJUDICE"; papers so marked must not be shown to or read by the court;
- Any letters, bills, invoices, etc., between you and the creditor, or you and his solicitors, which are connected with the case, but are not exhibits to the witness statements.

THE PROCEDURE AT THE HEARING

The procedure at the hearing of the petition will be the same as it was at the hearing of application to set aside, except that the creditor (now called "**the petitioning creditor**") will now open, i.e. begin putting his case, and you will be responding to it.

Make a careful note of what he, or his lawyer, says, and of what the judge says. There may again be cross-examination of the witnesses, whose witness statements have been read, or there may be a witness or witnesses, who has or have not made witness statements, but are specially allowed by the court to give evidence by word of mouth.

NO SECOND BITE

The court may not allow any arguments by you, which failed on the hearing of your application to set aside, to be put forward again in opposition to the petition. The same rule applies to the petitioning creditor's arguments.

WHAT ORDERS WILL BE MADE

At the end of the hearing, the court will usually give judgment at once. If the petition succeeds, the court will make a bankruptcy order against you, and will also order the petitioning creditor's costs of the hearing to be assessed and added to his debt.

If you believe that you have a real possibility of paying off the debt and costs for which you can show some proof, so long as a bankruptcy order is not made, tell the petitioning creditor's lawyers, and the court, that you would like a short adjournment in which to pay, explaining how you are going to be able to do it.

DISQUALIFICATION CAUSED BY THE BANKRUPTCY ORDER

When a bankruptcy order is made against you, you are prohibited from exercising some of your civil rights, until you are discharged. This is called "Disqualification through Bankruptcy", page 51 below.

While you are disqualified, you commit a criminal offence if you exercise any of those rights, or try to exercise any of them.

THE DISQUALIFICATIONS

While you are an undischarged bankrupt, it is an offence, for which you can be prosecuted, for you:

(1) to be a Member of the House of Commons, or to sit or vote in the House of Lords;
(2) to be a director of a limited company, or to take part in promoting, forming or operating a company, without the permission of the bankruptcy court;
(3) to act as receiver or manager of a company for debenture-holders of a company.

Other disqualifications apply to a bankrupt who, although discharged, has had a "**bankruptcy restrictions order**" made against him, or has had to give a "**bankruptcy restrictions undertaking**"; see Chapter 22, page 95 below.

There are many other minor disqualifications from holding office, after becoming bankrupt.

For discharges, see Chapter 22, below.

APPEAL

You are entitled to appeal against any order made against you, for which you need the court's permission. You should ask the court to "stay", that is, suspend, the operation of the bankruptcy order, such as the advertisement of it in the press, while you appeal. The court will usually put you under stiff conditions for granting this, and will ask you the grounds on which you want to appeal against its judgment. Your appeal will need to be filed **within 21 days of the date of the decision**. For this, you will need the assistance of a lawyer. You can be assisted by the CAB and/or by the court officials, although the advice of a lawyer would often be desirable: see Chapter 25.

CHAPTER 14

HOW THE BANKRUPTCY ORDER AFFECTS YOU

The court has now made a bankruptcy order against you. This order takes effect the moment it is made; the exact time is noted by the judge. The order requires you to visit the Official Receiver straightaway at his office, which is open from 10.00 a.m. until 4.00 p.m.

If the court adds any conditions to the order, such as postponing the advertisement of the order, the order will state this. When you see the Official Receiver, he will give you a copy of the order, which he will at once advertise, unless the court has ordered the postponement of the advertisement.

You must from now on carry out all the Official Receiver's orders and instructions; if you do not, you may be brought before the court, and risk being sent to prison for contempt of court, and/or prosecuted. But if you work in well with him and your trustee in bankruptcy, life can be much easier for you: see the next paragraph.

WHETHER THE OFFICIAL RECEIVER NEEDS TO INVESTIGATE YOUR AFFAIRS

The Official Receiver is, in general, under a duty, if he thinks it necessary, to investigate your affairs in some detail, in the ways set out below. But he may decide that your affairs do not need investigating, or that the investigation can be carried out very quickly.

If he forms this view during the first year after your bankruptcy order, he can file a notice with the court to state that. If he does file such a notice, you will be discharged from your bankruptcy from the date when the notice was filed. A copy of the notice is printed in the Appendix at page 197, below.

MAKING YOUR STATEMENT OF AFFAIRS

The Official Receiver will ask you to complete your **statement of affairs,** for which he will give you the forms, and a booklet of instructions on how to fill them out; they are lengthy. This has to be a complete statement of all your property, of every sort, and of all your debts. You must complete it **within 21 days after the date of the bankruptcy order.**

You can, if you have some good reasons, ask the Official Receiver to let you off making a statement of affairs altogether, or to allow you more time for completing it. If he refuses to let you off, or to allow you more time, you can apply to the court for a release, or for more time to complete the statement. This will be an ordinary application (Form 7.2), fee £30.

If you cannot complete the statement of affairs by yourself, the Official Receiver can be asked to agree to employ someone to help you with it, without cost to yourself; the expenses will be collected out of your property. Or you yourself may employ someone to help you with it, and ask the Official Receiver for a contribution towards the expenses of doing so.

When the statement is completed, you will have to sign it, and the Official Receiver will make you confirm it on affidavit, that, is, swear an oath that it is true and correct; see Chapter 9, page 31, above.

PREPARING YOUR ACCOUNTS

The Official Receiver may ask you to prepare accounts of your affairs, in whatever form and for whatever period he specifies. Basically, the accounts will have to go back for three years before the bankruptcy order, but they may be asked for going further back.

You can also ask the Official Receiver for help with doing these accounts, and with meeting the expenses of preparing them. Two copies of the accounts, confirmed again by affidavit, must be delivered to the

Official Receiver, **within 21 days from the time when he asked for them,** or such longer time as he may agree.

MAKING FURTHER STATEMENTS

In addition to your statement of affairs, and your accounts, the Official Receiver may ask for further information about your affairs, to be provided by you in writing. He will ask for this, so as to expand, alter or explain what you have said in your statement of affairs, or what you have put in your accounts. Two copies of this further statement, signed by you, must be delivered to the Official Receiver, **within 21 days after he has asked for it,** or within such longer period as he may allow. It must also be confirmed on affidavit, if he so requires.

DISQUALIFICATIONS CAUSED BY THE BANKRUPTCY ORDER

For the disqualifications affecting your personal, business and public life caused by the bankruptcy order, see Chapter 13, page 49, above.

THE FIRST MEETING OF CREDITORS

Within four months after the bankruptcy order, the Official Receiver may decide to summon the first meeting of your creditors, of which you will be given notice. If asked to attend the meeting, you must do so, and at the meeting you must answer any questions allowed by the chairman to be put to you by the creditors. If you are asked to attend any further meetings, you must do so. If he decides not to summon a meeting of creditors, he must give the court and all creditors of whom he is aware notice of that. From the giving of that notice, he becomes the trustee himself.

The principal task of the first meeting of creditors is to appoint someone to be the **"trustee in bankruptcy"** of your **"bankruptcy estate"**, that is, of all your property: he must be a **"licensed insolvency practitioner"**: see Chapter 17, page 67 below.

YOUR DUTIES AND LIABILITIES TOWARDS YOUR CREDITORS

All the duties described above, which you must carry out as directed by the Official Receiver, and also as directed by the trustee in bankruptcy, must be carried out fully and sincerely.

If you fail, without a good excuse, to do what is required of you to their satisfaction, you run the risk of being brought before the court on a charge of contempt of court. You also risk the date of your discharge being suspended: see Chapter 22, below.

CHAPTER 15

THE COURT'S POWER TO EXAMINE YOU, YOUR FAMILY OR OTHER PEOPLE

The court has special powers to order you to be examined publicly, in court, about your affairs. This "public examination" is applied for by the Official Receiver. You have to go into the witness box, and answer on oath questions from the Official Receiver, the trustee in bankruptcy or any of your creditors; such examinations are not often ordered, except in bad cases.

The court also has the power to order your "private examination". Under this procedure, you are questioned privately (i.e. not in open court), again on oath, about your affairs; this can be applied for by the Official Receiver or by the trustee in bankruptcy.

They can also apply for the private examination of your wife, husband, civil partner or partner, business partner, or any other person whom they believe to have important information about your affairs, your assets or your debts. Answers which you give at such examinations may be used against you, and their answers can be used against them, in other legal proceedings.

If you, or members of your family, are summoned to any such public or private examination, you or they must attend very punctually, and be sure to bring whatever papers or documents the summons to attend tells you to bring with you.

CHAPTER 16

CRIMINAL OFFENCES WITH WHICH A BANKRUPT CAN BE CHARGED

A person who has been made bankrupt can be prosecuted for a large number of offences, arising from what he has done, or not done, during the period before the bankruptcy order. Details of these are set out below.

The statutory defence

Grounds of defence can be raised in answer to prosecutions for many of such offences; these are set out, at page 65, below, at the end of the list of offences.

The bankrupt commits an offence by doing, or by failing to do, any of the following things:

(A) Disclosure of property and of any disposals

If he does, or has done, any of the following things:

(1) if he does not, to the best of his knowledge and belief, disclose to the Official Receiver or the trustee in bankruptcy all of his property that belongs to his "bankruptcy estate", that is, all the property which by the bankruptcy order is taken away from him and given to his trustee for distribution among his creditors;

Note: The property here referred to includes his after-acquired property (see Chapter 17, below) and those items of his personal property which have more than their replacement value (see Chapter 18, below).

(2) if he does not inform the Official Receiver or the trustee in bankruptcy of any property which has been disposed of, and which, if not so disposed of, would have formed part of his bankruptcy estate, stating, how, when, to whom and for what value it was disposed of.

Note: This offence does not include any property disposed of by the bankrupt in the course of carrying on his business, or any payment of his ordinary expenses or those of his family.

(B) Concealment or removal of property

(1) if he does not deliver up possession to the Official Receiver or to the trustee in bankruptcy, or as either of them direct him to deliver it, of any property forming part of his bankruptcy estate which is in his possession, or under his control, of which he is legally bound to deliver up possession.

(2) if he conceals any debt due to or from him, or any property worth not less than £1,000, possession of which he is legally bound to deliver up to the Official Receiver or the trustee in bankruptcy.

(3) He also commits an offence, if he did any of the things set out in paragraph (2) in the twelve months before the petition was presented, or in the period between the presentation of the petition and the making of the bankruptcy order, which would have been an offence, under paragraph (2), above, if the bankruptcy order had been made just before he did those things.

(4) if he removes, or during the period between the presentation of the petition and the making of the bankruptcy order he removed, any property worth not less than £1,000, possession of which he has been required, or possession of which he would have been required, to deliver up to the Official Receiver or the trustee in bankruptcy.

(5) if, after being required by the Official Receiver or the trustee in bankruptcy to account for the loss of any substantial part of his property during the twelve months before the presentation of the petition, or between the presentation of the petition and the making of the bankruptcy order, he fails, without reasonable excuse, to account for that loss, or to give a satisfactory explanation of how it was incurred.

(C) Concealment, falsification or destruction of books, papers, etc.

(1) if he does not deliver up to the Official Receiver or to the trustee in bankruptcy, or as either of them directs, all the books, papers and other records in his possession or control, relating to his bankruptcy estate or his affairs;

(2) if he prevents, or in the period between the presentation of the petition and the making of the bankruptcy order he prevented, the production of any books, papers or records relating to his bankruptcy estate or his affairs.

(3) if he conceals, destroys, mutilates or falsifies, or causes or permits the concealment, destruction, mutilation or falsification of, any books, papers or other records relating to his bankruptcy estate or his affairs;

(4) if he makes, or causes or permits the making of, any false entries in any book, document, or record relating to his bankruptcy estate or his affairs;

Note: "Records", for the purposes of the above offences, includes the data stored within a computer owned, controlled or used by the bankrupt; it is therefore an offence to alter its database, or to wipe its memory.

(5) if, in the twelve months before the presentation of the petition, or in the period between the presentation of the petition and the making of the bankruptcy order, he did anything which would have been an offence under paragraphs (3) or (4) above, if the bankruptcy order had been made before he did it.

Note: In the case of a trading record, the above period of twelve months is increased to two years.

(6) if he disposes of, or alters or makes any omission in, or causes or permits the disposal, altering or making any omission in, any book, document or record relating to his bankruptcy estate or his affairs.

(7) if, in the twelve months before the presentation of the petition, or in the period between the presentation of the petition and the making of the bankruptcy order, he did anything described in paragraph (6), which would have been an offence, if the bankruptcy order had been made just before he did it.

Note: In the case of a trading record, the above period of twelve months increased to two years.

(D) False statements, failure to inform

(1) if he makes, or has made, any material omission in any statement he is required to make under the provisions of the statutes, relating to his affairs;

(2) if, knowing or believing that a false debt has been "proved", that is, claimed, by any person in his bankruptcy, he fails as soon as practicable to inform the trustee;

(3) if he attempts to account for any part of his property by pretended losses or expenses;

(4) if, at any meeting of his creditors in the twelve months before the presentation of the petition, or (whether or not at any such meeting) at any time during the period between the presentation of the petition and the making of the bankruptcy order, he did anything which would have been an offence under paragraph (3), above, if the bankruptcy order had been made just before he did it;

(5) if he is, or at any time has been, guilty of any false representation or other fraud for the purpose of obtaining the consent of his creditors, or any of them, to an agreement with reference to his affairs or to his bankruptcy;

(E) Fraudulent disposal or concealment of property

(1) if he makes or causes to be made or, within the five years before the bankruptcy order, he made or caused to be made, any gift or transfer of, or any charge on, his property, or caused or connived at the levying of any execution against his property;

Note: "Conniving" here means helping with the execution or its carrying out, and indicates that what the bankrupt did with reference to the execution was dishonest.

The very severe terms of this offence are reduced by "the Statutory Defence" (see below).

(2) if he conceals or removes or, at any time before the making of the bankruptcy order, he concealed or removed any part of his

property after, or within two months before, the date of a judgment or order given or made against him, which judgment or order was not "satisfied", that is, paid up in full, before the bankruptcy order;

(F) Absconding, that is, leaving England and Wales

(1) if he leaves, or attempts or prepares to leave, England and Wales with any property, worth not less than £1,000, possession of which he is required to deliver up to the Official Receiver or the trustee in bankruptcy.

(2) he also commits an offence if, in the six months before the presentation of the petition, or between the presentation of the petition and the making of the bankruptcy order, he does anything which would have been an offence under paragraph (1), above, if the bankruptcy order had been made just before he did it;

(G) Fraudulent dealing with property obtained on credit

(1) if, in the twelve months before the presentation of the petition, or between the presentation of the petition and the making of the bankruptcy order, he disposed of, or pawned or pledged, any property obtained by him on credit, for which, at the time of disposing of it, he had not paid, regard being had to the price received for the property.

Warning to purchasers from bankrupts: It should be noted that a person is guilty of any offence, if, in the twelve months before the presentation of the petition, or between the presentation of the petition and the making of the bankruptcy order, he acquired or received property from the bankrupt, knowing or believing that the bankrupt owed money in respect of the property, and that the bankrupt did not intend, or was unlikely to be able, to pay the money he owed on the property, regard being had to the price that person paid for the property.

(H) Obtaining credit: engaging in business

(1) if, alone or jointly with another person, he obtains credit of £500 or more, without informing the person from whom he obtains

the credit that he is an undischarged bankrupt, or that, though discharged, he is subject to a bankruptcy restrictions order or a bankruptcy restrictions undertaking (see Chapter 22, below).

Note: "Obtaining credit" here includes (a) obtaining goods bailed to him under a hire-purchase agreement, or agreed to be sold by him under a conditional sale agreement, and (b) where he is paid in advance, whether in money or otherwise, for the supply of goods or services.

What are offences no longer:

The former law now repealed made it an offence:

(1) for a bankrupt (a) while engaged in business in the two years before the presentation of the petition, not to have kept proper accounting records of his business for that period, and for any part of the period between the presentation of the petition and the making of the bankruptcy order during which he was carrying on business; or (b) not to have preserved the accounting records which he had kept;

(2) for a bankrupt (a) in the two years before the presentation of the petition, to have materially contributed to, or increased the state of, his insolvency, by gambling or by rash and hazardous speculations; or (b) during the period between the presentation of the petition and the making of the bankruptcy order, to have lost any part of his property by gambling or rash and hazardous speculations; the extent to which the speculations could be held to be rash and hazardous depended on the bankrupt's financial position at the time he entered into them.

Note: Although these offences no longer exist, a bankrupt who has not kept, and has not preserved, proper accounts of his business, or has engaged in gambling or in rash and hazardous speculations to the extent set out above, is still liable to be penalised by the court on those grounds, in relation to the possible suspension of his discharge, or in deciding whether to make a bankruptcy restrictions order against him: see Chapter 22, page 97, below.

THE STATUTORY DEFENCE TO BANKRUPTCY OFFENCES

In relation to some of the offences listed above, the statute makes the following defence available to the bankrupt:

"Defence of innocent intention"

"A person is not guilty of the offence, if he proves that, at the time of the conduct constituting the offence, he had no intention to defraud or to conceal the state of his affairs" (Insolvency Act 1986, s. 352).

This defence is available to a bankrupt in the case of the following offences, listed above:

Paragraphs (A) (1) – (2), (B) (1) – (5), (C) (1) – (7), (D) (1), (E) (1) – (2).

CHAPTER 17

THE TRUSTEE IN BANKRUPTCY: HIS POWERS OVER YOU AND YOUR PROPERTY

Unless the Official Receiver has become the trustee in bankruptcy (see Chapter 15, p. 57, above) he will have called the first meeting of creditors who will vote to appoint an official, an accountant or a solicitor, called a "licensed insolvency practitioner" to be "the trustee in bankruptcy".

The trustee becomes the trustee, i.e. the legal owner, of what is called "your bankruptcy estate", that means, all the property which you owned at the time of the bankruptcy order, and also some sorts of property which you have come to own, or will come to own later on, during the bankruptcy. He is also in charge of all the debts that you owe. All these things it will be his duty to manage.

But he does not just manage your property; he actually becomes the legal owner of nearly all of it, and you cease to be the owner of practically any of it. As soon as the creditors at their meeting have appointed him, he becomes the owner.

In the past, bankrupts used to complain that their trustees in bankruptcy were inefficient and unfair to them, and that they did not make the best realisations of the bankrupt's property, and that their fees, payable out of the bankrupt's property, were too high, and their expenses too large. The new profession of licensed insolvency practitioners now consists of properly trained and experienced professionals, who are licensed and controlled by their professional bodies, the Department of Trade and Industry and the Insolvency Service, to deal with the administration of bankruptcies and wound-up companies in winding-up.

So you should not have much cause to complain of your trustee's management. But if you are not satisfied, with good reason, with it or him, or with the fees and expenses he is charging or has charged, you can complain to the authorities, or to the court.

When the Official Receiver becomes the trustee in bankruptcy, his fees and expenses are regulated by the rules.

There are exceptions to what sorts of property the trustee in bankruptcy comes to own straightaway, on his appointment; there are some things he comes to own later, and some things that he can never own at all: see Chapters 18, 19 and 20, below.

IMPORTANCE OF YOUR RELATIONS WITH THE TRUSTEE IN BANKRUPTCY

Just as you were advised above, with reference to your dealings with the Official Receiver, to do, and do willingly, everything he asks you to do, and to keep on good terms with him, so it should be with the trustee in bankruptcy. He can ask you to do things, to advise him about your property and your business transactions, and to answer questions, all of which you must do. His goodwill can be of great assistance to you during the bankruptcy.

In particular, you do not wish to give him any cause to support any application by the Official Receiver for the suspension of your discharge (see Chapter 22, below). His goodwill can be important in relation to his right to demand a "swap" of any of your business goods, equipment, cars, etc., of "excess value" (see Chapter 18, below), and in relation to the possibility of you and your family continuing to occupy the matrimonial home, instead of it being disposed of: (see Chapter 20, below).

His attitude towards you could be important from another aspect, if it is later thought to be possible to convert your bankruptcy into an "individual voluntary arrangement", which he would need to support and to conduct, as a result of which your bankruptcy order would be annulled: see Chapter 24, page 107 below.

CHAPTER 18

YOUR RIGHTS AS TO YOUR PROPERTY, YOUR FURNITURE AND YOUR MEANS OF LIVELIHOOD

The general take-over by the trustee in bankruptcy of your property is subject to the following exceptions:

(1) *The equipment which you need for carrying on your business, doing your job or following your profession*

The trustee in bankruptcy is not entitled, as of right, to any of the tools, books, vehicles or other equipment which you need to use personally in your employment, business or vocation, that is, your profession. But he may have a right to "demand a swap" of some items, if they are "of excess value", as explained in paragraph (5), below. He could very well require your car, if of high value, to be handed over for sale, and replaced by a cheaper model. Whether a high-value computer could similarly be claimed and sold must depend on the nature of its use, and the contents of its database.

See under paragraph (7), below, as to the carrying on of a business by you, as a bankrupt, and see also Chapter 19, below.

(2) *Your domestic furniture, etc.*

The trustee in bankruptcy is not entitled to your clothing, furniture, household equipment or provisions, which you have the right to retain, to the extent necessary to satisfy the basic domestic needs of yourself and your family.

This does not prevent him from claiming, as he must, your personal jewellery, other than your wedding ring, and would not prevent him from claiming, perhaps, some items out of an excessive number of suits in your wardrobe, or the contents of your wine cellar, if containing a number of bottles of vintage wine, capable of being profitably sold. Valuable paintings or other pictures or works of art would certainly be claimed.

(3) *Property which you hold in trust for another person*

If you are yourself a trustee of any property which you hold for some one else, and in which you own no personal interest, (apart, perhaps, from being repaid for any expenses you have incurred), that property does not pass to the trustee.

(4) *Property subject to orders under the Proceeds of Crime Act 2002*

If you should have unfortunately become subject to orders made under the Proceeds of Crime Act 2002, or the earlier confiscation statutes, before the bankruptcy order, for the seizure of any of your property so as to recover "the proceeds of crime", or "the profits from a criminal life-style", that property cannot be claimed by the trustee, until those proceedings have finished. But if the orders were made after the making of the bankruptcy order, then they cannot apply to any of your bankruptcy estate, for the trustee in bankruptcy's claim then takes precedence.

(5) *The trustee in bankruptcy's right "to demand a swap"*

Where the trustee in bankruptcy thinks that the realisable value or values of any or all of the items of your property described in paragraphs (1) or (2), above, is or are greater than the cost of reasonable replacements of that property or any part of it, he may give you notice in writing that he claims that property, or that part of it, for the bankrupt's estate.

The words "a reasonable replacement" mean that the item bought as a replacement is reasonably adequate for meeting the needs previously met by the property it is replacing.

The trustee in bankruptcy must give you notice of his claims within a period of 42 days, beginning with the day when he first came to know of the property in question; but the court can extend that period: but it will not do so, if the trustee has allowed an unreasonable period of time to run, (such as several years), before making his claim.

The receipt by you of that notice, when "served" on you by the trustee in bankruptcy, passes the property in question to him as part of the bankruptcy estate, as if it had always been part of that estate.

How the replacement process works

The trustee in bankruptcy may buy the replacement items, before he has sold the original items; but he is not obliged to buy the replacement items, until he has enough funds in hand in the bankruptcy estate to pay for them. A member of your family, or a friend, may offer to pay the trustee in bankruptcy a sum of money equal to what he would receive by selling the original items, and purchasing replacements; the trustee in bankruptcy may accept the offer, if he thinks it to be reasonable. If his refusal is seriously unreasonable, application to the court could be made, to order him to accept the offer.

(6) *Certain tenancies of houses, flats or land*

Subject to certain conditions, the trustee in bankruptcy cannot, as of right, claim from you, as the bankrupt, as forming part of the bankruptcy estate, the following tenancies: an assured tenancy, an assured agricultural tenancy, a protected tenancy, the tenancy of a house of which you are the protected occupier, or a secure tenancy. But he can give you a notice in writing claiming it, and when you receive the notice, the tenancy automatically becomes part of the bankruptcy estate, as if it had always been so.

(7) *"After-acquired property"*

The trustee in bankruptcy is entitled to claim from you any property (a) which you have acquired after the date of the bankruptcy order, and (b) any property which has devolved on you, that is, has come into your possession, such as a legacy under a will, after that date.

Your duties with respect to after-acquired property

Where you acquire after-acquired property, as described above, or any such property devolves on you, or where there is an increase in your income (see Chapter 19, page 73 below), it is your duty to give the trustee in bankruptcy notice of that property, or of that increase, **within 21 days** of your becoming aware of it. Having given that notice, you must not dispose of the property for a **period of 42 days** from the date of your notice.

If you have failed to give the trustee in bankruptcy the required notice, or if you have disposed of the property before the expiry of the above period of 42 days, you must immediately inform the trustee in bankruptcy of what you have done, and of the name and address of the person to whom you disposed of the property, and all other information he may need, to enable him to trace it and recover it from that person, if they are not protected from such a claim.

Where you are carrying on a business

Where, after the bankruptcy order, you are carrying on a business, you must, not less often than every six months, inform the trustee in bankruptcy about it, showing the total of goods bought and sold, or services supplied, and the profit or loss arising from the carrying on of the business. The trustee in bankruptcy may require you to provide him with more, or more frequent, information, including accounts of the business.

How the trustee in bankruptcy claims after-acquired property

The trustee in bankruptcy makes his claim by serving you with a notice in writing; when you receive the notice, the property referred to in the notice passes to the trustee in bankruptcy, and automatically becomes part of the bankruptcy estate, as if it had always formed part of that estate.

Exceptions to claims for after-acquired property

The trustee may not claim, as after-acquired property, any of the excepted property listed in paragraphs (1) and (2), above, nor any other property which under any other statute is protected from such claims, nor any of your income; monies payable to you as part of your income can only be claimed from you by means of "an income payments order", or under "an income payments agreement"; this would include the takings from your business: see above, and Chapter 19, page 73 below.

If some other person, in good faith, and for value, not knowing that you were a bankrupt, has bought any of your after-acquired property from you, the trustee in bankruptcy cannot claim it from them, nor can he claim any money from a banker who has dealt with you in good faith, not knowing that you were a bankrupt.

CHAPTER 19

YOUR RIGHTS TO YOUR INCOME AFTER BANKRUPTCY: INCOME PAYMENTS ORDERS AND AGREEMENTS

As explained in Chapter 18, a bankrupt's earned income, whether received by way of wages, salary or piecework, or from the carrying on of a business (so far as that is legally possible for him) do not automatically pass to his trustee in bankruptcy. No bankrupt, it has been said, should be a slave to his creditors. But being a bankrupt you may still be required to make contributions to the bankruptcy estate out of your income, for distribution among your creditors.

To collect those contributions, the trustee in bankruptcy has two means available to him.

(1) He may apply to the court to make "an income payments order" against you. This will require you to pay to him, or require the person who pays you, to pay to him, over a specified period, a part or a proportion of your net earnings, in whatever form or in respect of whatever period they are payable to you.

(2) *Alternatively*, he may ask you to agree to enter into "an income payments agreement": see **"Income payments agreements"**, below.

What is your "income"?

Your income, for this purpose, is described in the statute as follows:

"Every payment in the nature of income, which is from time to time made [to you], or to which [you] from time to time become entitled, including any payment in respect of the carrying on of any business, or in respect of an office or employment, and any payment under a pension scheme, except payments by way of guaranteed minimum pension, or payments giving effect to [your] protected rights as a member of a pension scheme".

Any pension payments which you were receiving before the bankruptcy order, other than the excluded ones mentioned above, automatically pass to the trustee in bankruptcy without any order; for they are not income derived from office, employment or the carrying on of business.

The application for an income payments order

The trustee in bankruptcy will apply to the court, which will fix a venue (that is, a place, date and time, for hearing his application). The trustee must give you **at least 28 days notice of the hearing**, and must send you a copy of his application, and a short statement of his grounds for making it.

Unless you send to the court and to the trustee in bankruptcy, **at least 7 days before the date of the hearing**, your written consent to the terms of the income payments order which is proposed, you must attend the hearing. When you do, you will have the right to explain to the court why you think that the order should not be made, or should not be made in the form proposed by the trustee in bankruptcy.

The making of an income payments order

When an order is made, the trustee must send you a sealed copy of it. If the order is for the payments to be made by some person or company other than yourself, a sealed copy of the order must be sent to them. An order for payments to be made by another person or company will generally not be made, unless you have failed to obey the order, and make the payments as required.

Where the trustee needs the court to make such an order for payment by another person or company, the trustee will apply to the court for it, without notice to yourself or that other person or company. If such an order is later varied, the trustee must send a sealed copy of it to that other person or company.

When that person or company receives notice of such an order having been made, he or it must immediately arrange for the payments to be made as ordered. He or it will be entitled to deduct from each sum payable the sum of 50p, as a contribution to the clerical and administrative costs of making the payment.

Where that person or company is not liable to make any payments of income to you, or has made all the payments to you which are required to be made, he or it must give notice to the trustee in bankruptcy.

Duration of order

The trustee in bankruptcy may only apply for an income payments order before the date of your discharge; although the order he obtains may remain in force against you after your discharge. But the order may not remain in force for more than three years from the date it was made.

Limitation on the amount of the order

The court cannot make an order, the effect of which would be to reduce your income, when taken together with certain pension payments which you may be receiving, below what appears to the court to be necessary for meeting the reasonable domestic needs of you and your family.

The terms of the order

The order will either require you, or the person who, or the company which, pays you, to pay to the trustee in bankruptcy the sum specified in the order. If, after the court has made an order that you should make such payments, you fail to do so, the court will make an order that the person, or the company paying you, shall pay. The person, or the company paying you, is not involved in the application for the order, or in its making; but if an order is made against him or it, he or it will be sent a copy of the order, which they will be legally bound to carry out.

Attachment of Earnings order

If, when an income payments order is being applied for, you are already subject to an attachment of earnings order, under which you have to make payments, you or the trustee in bankruptcy may apply to the court for it to be discharged.

Review or discharge of the income payments order

When an income payments order has been made, either the trustee in bankruptcy or you yourself may apply to the court for it to be reviewed or discharged. When the trustee in bankruptcy applies, he must follow the procedure as described above for his original application.

When you are applying to review or discharge the income payments order, you will be applying at first without notice to the trustee. The court will read your application, which you must support with a brief statement of your grounds for making it. If the court considers that you do not show sufficiently strong grounds for a review or discharge, it will dismiss your application, but not until it has given you a private hearing, of which it must give you **7 days' notice**. The fee for making the application is £30 or £60.

If the court considers that you do show sufficiently strong grounds, it will fix a venue (that is, a place, date and time) for you to make the application at a hearing attended by the trustee. You must then, **not less than 28 days before the hearing,** send the trustee in bankruptcy copies of your application and of your grounds for making it.

The trustee in bankruptcy may appear at the hearing, and take part in it. Whether he attends or not, he may send to the court and to you, **not less than 7 days before the date of the hearing,** a written report of any matters which he thinks should be brought to the court's attention.

Sealed copies of any order made on the application must be sent by the court to the trustee, to you and to any other person or company liable to make the payments.

Income payments agreements

Instead of applying to the court for an income payments order, the trustee in bankruptcy may ask you to enter into a written agreement with him, to the same effect, called "**an income payments agreement**"; he must send you a draft agreement to show you what he proposes and to obtain your agreement to it.

If you receive from the trustee in bankruptcy a draft income payments agreement, you must reply to him in writing **within 14 days (unless he has give you a longer period to consider it)**, saying whether you agree or disagree with his proposals. If you agree, you must sign the draft agreement and send it back to him with your reply. The statute does not refer to your proposing different terms or amounts, but you must presumably be entitled to do so.

When the trustee in bankruptcy receives the agreement signed by you, he will sign and date it, and it then comes into force at once. If the agreement provides for the payments to be made by a person or company other than yourself, the trustee in bankruptcy must send them a notice of the making of the agreement, which must state:

(a) Their full name and address;
(b) Your full name and address;
(c) The full name and address of the trustee in bankruptcy, to whom the payments are to be made;
(d) A statement that an income payments agreement has been made, giving its date, and how much they have to pay to the trustee in bankruptcy out of the sums they owe you, giving the amounts payable, the intervals at which they are to be payable, and the period over which they are to be payable, and allowing them to deduct the sum of 50p from each payment as a contribution to clerical and administrative costs.

Duration of agreement

See "**Duration of order**", at page 75, above.

Attachment of Earnings order

See note above at page 76.

Where the payments made under the order or the agreement go

All sums paid under the order or the agreement form part of the bankruptcy estate. The specific sums, or the proportion of what is owing to you, which is ordered or agreed to be paid by you, may be increased or decreased by the court on application by the trustee in bankruptcy or by yourself, whether before or after your discharge.

There is an official form (Form 6.81) for you to apply to the court to vary an income payments order: court fee £30.

CHAPTER 20

YOUR HOME: WHAT RIGHTS HAVE YOU AND YOUR FAMILY TO STAY IN OCCUPATION?

Note: A new law, called the Civil Partnership Act 2004, has been passed, to give the "civil partners" to a "civil partnership", which has been duly registered, the same rights and make them subject to the same duties and obligations, as apply to married couples. The law came into force on 5th December 2005. It appears that the Government now proposes to give unmarried couples of opposite sex the same rights.

Your home is often called in the law the "matrimonial home", even when you and your partner with whom you share it are not married. If you and your partner are "civil partners", in a "civil partnership" registered under the Civil Partnership Act 2004 (see above), your home is now to be called "the civil partnership home".

Your home is usually the most valuable thing which you and your partner (if a part-owner with you) possess. You will almost certainly have mortgaged it to a bank or a building society. When you are bankrupt, they, and the trustee in bankruptcy, will want to get possession of it and sell it. This can be postponed for a time, if someone with enough cash or security can take over the mortgage payments, which would leave you in occupation; it can be completely stopped, if someone could take over the mortgage entirely, and the mortgage debt.

In what follows, when a house is referred to, this includes a flat, although there are special problems with a flat, which can rarely be owned as a freehold.

In earlier times, the home, whether freehold or rented, was almost always in the name of the husband. When he became bankrupt, his wife was liable to be evicted, as she had no legal interest in the house which allowed her to stay there.

Nowadays, the great majority of homes are owned in the joint names of husband and wife, or, if they are not married, in the joint names of the partners. If they are not married, they do not yet enjoy the special protection which the law gives to married partners (and has now given also to civil partners); but they are not subject to some of the obligations imposed on civil partners.

There are, of course, other patterns of family occupation: a father or a mother may share the ownership of the house, or its occupation, with a son or daughter or other relation, or an aunt may share a home with a niece. Such joint occupations do not enjoy those privileges either.

Persons may own a house jointly either as "joint tenants", that is, they jointly own the whole property in the house, or as "tenants in common", in which case they each own one undivided half of the property in the house. Ownership as joint tenants has so far been by far the commoner form of ownership; it has the advantage that when one of the tenants dies, the other joint tenant inherits their joint share automatically, although this rule no longer applies fully in bankruptcy.

But the great increases in the value of houses are making very many people liable to inheritance tax. Many joint home owners are now being advised by financial or tax advisers to change their form of home ownership from being joint tenants to being tenants in common.

What happens to your rights of occupation after the bankruptcy order?

When you are made bankrupt, your joint halfshare, or your "tenancy in common", in the house passes to the trustee in bankruptcy, subject of course to any mortgage on the house. The value of the equity, that is, the sale value of your share of the house after paying off the mortgage, will when realised be divided up among your creditors.

Any legal proceedings about a house involved in a bankruptcy must be heard by the Bankruptcy Court.

The trustee in bankruptcy has the right to apply to the court for an order that you, your wife, partner or civil partner, and your children, give up possession of the house, so that it may be sold. This is where the special rights, referred to above, come into play. These rights are given to the wife (or husband or civil partner) of a bankrupt, or to their previous wife or husband or civil partner, with regard to the bankrupt, his wife (or her husband), or civil partner remaining in occupation of the house.

The rights of occupation of "co-owners"

Where your wife, husband, civil partner or partner, is a co-owner with you, who are a bankrupt, they, being either a joint tenant or a tenant in common, have legal rights to occupy, or to return to, the house, and they cannot be evicted from it, or excluded from returning to it, except by an order of the court.

On an application by the trustee in bankruptcy for such an order, the court has to take into consideration the following matters:

(a) the interests of your creditors;
(b) the conduct of your wife (or former wife or former civil partner) or of your husband (or former husband or former civil partner), in so far as they have contributed to the bankruptcy;
(c) her (or his) needs and financial resources;
(d) the needs of any children;
(e) all the circumstances of the case, other than the needs of yourself, the bankrupt.

"Contributing to the bankruptcy", in paragraph (b) above, is generally taken to mean that the other co-owner has taken part in luxurious living at the creditors' expense. This aspect may present difficulties of proof, or rather disproof.

Limitation to twelve months

See this heading, at page 83, below.

"Matrimonial home rights" now "home rights" of wife or husband or civil partner

Your wife or husband (called in the statute "the spouse"), who is not a joint tenant or a tenant in common, but who is, or is entitled to be, in occupation of the matrimonial home (or the home in a civil partnership), has what until now have been called **"matrimonial home rights"**, now to be called just **"home rights"**, which prevent her, or him, from being evicted from the home or excluded from returning to it, except by order of a court. A civil partner has those rights, but an unmarried partner does not have these rights at present, but may get them in the future.

Your rights of occupation as the bankrupt

You yourself, as the bankrupt, have the right of occupation of any house, and the right not to be excluded from returning to any house, in respect of which you have (or had, before the bankruptcy order) the right to occupy and the right not to be excluded from it, except by order of a court.

Rights of occupation of children under 18

If you were occupying the house, both at the date of the presentation of the petition and at the date of the bankruptcy order, and had children under the age of 18 living with you during that period, for whom the house was their home, they also have the right to occupy it and not to be evicted or excluded from it, whether or not your wife or your husband or civil partner has home rights, except by order of a court.

This helps to protect the position of a single or divorced parent, with whom the children live.

Where your wife or civil partner or husband or civil partner is not a co-owner: their rights

Where your wife or husband or civil partner (or former wife or husband or civil partner) is not a co-owner, but has home rights, (see above), they cannot be evicted from or excluded from the matrimonial home, or the civil partnership home, except by an order of the Bankruptcy Court.

In deciding whether to make against such a person such order as it thinks just and reasonable, the court must have regard to the following factors:

a) the interests of your creditors;
b) his or her conduct as your wife or husband or civil partner, or former wife, or former husband or former civil partner, in contributing to the bankruptcy (see above);
c) his or her needs and financial resources;
d) the needs of any children;
e) all the circumstances of the case, except your own needs as the bankrupt.

Limitation of rights to twelve months: "exceptional circumstances"

Where an application to obtain possession of the matrimonial home or the civil partnership home is made by the trustee in bankruptcy **after twelve months from the date of the bankruptcy order**, the court must assume that the interests of your creditors are more important than the interests of yourself, the bankrupt, and of your wife or husband or civil partner, and of the children, **"unless the circumstances of the case are exceptional"**.

Exceptional circumstances

Decisions by the courts on what may be regarded as "exceptional circumstances" are at present not very encouraging for the bankrupt and his or her wife or civil partner and children. They have been limited to cases where the bankrupt, or his wife or her husband, was very ill, or where the family needed more time, either to move to another place to live, or to raise the money to buy out the trustee in bankruptcy's interest in their present one. Disturbance to the children's school attendance commitments, resulting from the family having to move out of area, is only very rarely accepted as an exceptional circumstance.

Your rights in connection with the realisation of your house

You have special rights in connection with a house or houses (which will be referred to collectively as "the house") which, at the date of the bankruptcy order, formed part of the bankruptcy estate, and was or were the sole or principal home or homes of yourself, and/or of your wife or husband or civil partner, and/or of your former wife or former husband or former civil partner.

At the end of three years from the date of the bankruptcy order (or at the end of an extended period: see below), unless the trustee in bankruptcy has taken one of the steps mentioned below, the house will cease to form part of the bankruptcy estate, and will automatically belong to you again. No deed or conveyance is necessary for this to happen.

Extension of three-year period

If you have not informed the trustee in bankruptcy of the existence of the house within three months from the date of the bankruptcy order, the period of three years only begins to run from the time when he is told of it by you, or he comes to know of it from other sources.

The period of three years may also be extended by the court, if it thinks it right to do so.

The steps, the taking of one of which by the trustee in bankruptcy will stop the house coming back to you by this means, are the following:

- where the trustee in bankruptcy sells the house, or
- where he applies for an order for its sale, or
- where he applies for an order for possession of it, or
- where he applies to the court for a "charging order" over it, or
- where you and he have agreed that you accept liability for payment of a specific sum of money (with or without interest), in exchange for which the house will cease to form part of the bankruptcy estate, (and will therefore come back to you).

What the trustee has to do about the house

When the three-year period has nearly ended, without the trustee in bankruptcy having taken any of those steps, he must give notice on an official form (Form 6.83) to you, and/or where appropriate and necessary also to your wife or husband or civil partner, and/or to your former wife or former husband or former civil partner. This notice must be given **not later than 14 days before the end of the three-year period,** or such other period as applies, (see above).

The notice must give details of the house, and, if it is registered land, must give its registration number. Where the house consists of registered land, he must apply to register it in your name; where it is unregistered land, he must give you a certificate as to it passing to you, on an official form (Form 6.84).

Where the house had been the sole or principal home of your wife or husband or civil partner, or of your former wife or former husband or former civil partner, the trustee in bankruptcy must also inform them that he has applied for such registration, or has given such a certificate.

If the trustee in bankruptcy thinks that for the house to remain part of the bankruptcy estate is of no benefit to creditors, and that its administration would be more efficient if it belonged to you, and gives you notice of his view to that effect, he must, instead of having to act at the end of the three-year period described above, carry out all the necessary steps **within one month from the date of his notice to you.**

Where the trustee in bankruptcy's applications are dismissed

If the trustee in bankruptcy makes an application to the court, either for sale, or for possession of the house, or for a charging order, before the end of the three-year period, and his application is dismissed, then unless the court orders otherwise, the house will automatically cease to be part of the bankruptcy estate, and will belong to you again.

Where the trustee in bankruptcy applies for an order against a "low value home"

Where the trustee in bankruptcy applies to the court, in the case of such a house as is described above, for an order for its sale, or for possession of it, or for a charging order over it, and it is shown to have a net value of not more than £1000, the court must dismiss the application. The net value is to be calculated by excluding from the gross value the amounts of any loans of money secured on the house by mortgage or charge, any other third party interest, and the reasonable costs of sale.

WHERE THE HOUSE IS SOUGHT TO BE REPOSSESSED AND SOLD BY A BANK, A BUILDING SOCIETY OR SOME OTHER HOLDER OF A CHARGE

Where a share in a jointly-owned house has been mortgaged or charged by one of the co-owners, and the mortgagee seeks to obtain an order for a sale of the house to realise the value of the share over which it has a charge, the court is no longer so strongly required as it used to be, under the former law, to make such an order. The court is now required to look carefully at the relationships of the parties, and consider what is the fair course to pursue.

CHAPTER 21

YOUR PAST TRANSACTIONS MAY BE RE-OPENED BY THE TRUSTEE IN BANKRUPTCY

An important part of the job of the trustee in bankruptcy is to look into the business and financial transactions which you entered into before the bankruptcy order was made. He has a duty to investigate, for the benefit of your creditors, whether any of the transactions, which you did within the periods specified below, broke any of the rules laid down by the bankruptcy law.

"Transactions at an undervalue", and "preferences"

Those rules deal

(a) with any transactions which were done by you, during those periods, "at an undervalue", that is, where you parted with more value out of your property than the value which you received or were to receive back, and

(b) with transactions which were done by you "by way of preference", where you made payments, or took other steps relating to your property, which were intended to prefer, that is, to do a favour to, one of your creditors, over and above the rest of them.

If the trustee in bankruptcy finds that there have been any such transactions or any such preferences, in breach of those rules, he can apply to the court to set them aside, or, by other means, to restore your financial position to what it would have been, if you had not done them: see **"Investigations by the trustee in bankruptcy"**, below.

Transactions at an undervalue

Three kinds of transactions at an undervalue are specified as being capable of being set aside by the court on the trustee's application:

1. Making a gift of a part of your property to someone, or entering into a transaction with someone, whereby you received no value from them in exchange for what you gave or provided to them;
2. Entering into a transaction with someone, "in consideration of marriage or of a civil partnership", that, is you gave them a part of your property, in return for their agreeing to marry you or to enter into a civil partnership with you, or for their agreeing to marry or enter into a civil partnership with someone else, such as your son or daughter;
3. Entering into a transaction with someone for a consideration, that is, for value in money or money's worth, which was "significantly less", that is, substantially less, than the value which they received from you.

Such transactions may, of course, also be preferences: see below.

Transactions by way of preference

These are transactions which were done by you, or allowed to be done by you, with one of your creditors, or with a person who was standing as surety for, or had given a guarantee for, any of your debts or liabilities.

In the eyes of the law, a preference is given, when you do, or suffer being done to you or your property, anything which has the effect of putting that person in a better position, should you later become bankrupt, than they would have been in, if that thing had not been done. But the court must be satisfied that when you did that thing, you were "influenced by a desire" to produce that effect for the benefit of that person. That desire does not have to be predominant.

However, if you gave such a preference to a person who was at the time "your associate", you will be regarded as having been influenced by such a desire to prefer, until the contrary is proved.

Who are your "associates"?

Your "associates", for the purposes of the statute, are the following persons:

Your wife, your husband, your civil partner, your relatives, the husbands and wives and civil partners of your relatives, and the husbands and wives and civil partners of the relatives of your wife or husband or civil partner.

"Relatives" includes brothers, sisters, uncles, aunts, lineal ancestors and lineal descendants (parent, grandparents, grandchildren, great-nephews, great-nieces, etc.), stepchildren, adopted children, and illegitimate children.

"Children" includes "children of the half-blood", that is, only one of whose parents falls into one of the above classes.

"Contingent liabilities" are existing liabilities to pay money, which may, but will not necessarily, turn into debts due from you. "Prospective liabilities" are liabilities which are likely to come into existence at a future date.

The terms "husband", "wife", and "civil partner" include former husbands, wives and civil partners, and also "reputed husbands and wives", and presumably also "reputed civil partners". A lover, to whom you are not married, and who is not your civil partner either, although not specifically included in these lists, might be brought in as a reputed wife or husband.

"Associate" also includes persons employed by you, or who employ you, or who at the time employed you, persons with whom you are or were at the time in partnership, persons who are the trustees of a trust of which you are a beneficiary, and persons who are beneficiaries of a trust of which you are a trustee (with certain exceptions).

Periods fixed for setting aside transactions at an undervalue and preferences

Transactions at an undervalue may be set aside by the court, **if made within a period of five years ending with the date of the presentation of the petition,** on which you were made bankrupt.

Transactions by way of preference of a creditor, which are not transactions at an undervalue, may also be set aside:

(a) if made with, or done for the benefit of, a person who was your "associate" (for the meaning of this, see above), **within a period of two years ending with that date;**

(b) if made with a person who was not your associate, **within a period of six months ending with that date.**

But transactions at an undervalue, if done by you **more than two years before, but less than five years before,** that date, and transactions done by you by way of preference, may not be set aside, unless (a) you were insolvent at the time of doing the, or (b) you became insolvent as a result of doing them.

Meaning of "insolvent"

"Insolvent" here means either (a) that you could not then pay all your debts as they fell due, or (b) that the value of your property was less than your debts and liabilities, including your contingent and prospective liabilities. "Contingent liabilities" and "prospective liabilities" are defined at page 89, above.

But if you did a transaction at an undervalue within those periods with a person who was your associate (see above), otherwise than through their being your employee, you will be presumed to have been insolvent at the time, until the contrary is proved.

Investigations by the trustee in bankruptcy

If the trustee in bankruptcy believes that you have engaged in transactions at an undervalue, or by way of preference of a creditor or guarantor, he can apply to the court for a private examination of you, or your wife, husband or civil partner, or of the persons with whom you did the transactions, or whom you are alleged to have preferred: see Chapter 15, above.

You and they can be compelled to answer questions on oath, and your answers can be used against you and their answers can be used against them, in later legal proceedings to set the transactions aside.

Consequences of having done transactions which can be set aside

If you have made a gift, during the period described above, and you fail to inform the trustee in bankruptcy of it, you commit an offence: see Chapter 16, above, offence (A) (2).

If you have done transactions capable of being set aside (and all the more likely, if they are set aside), those facts can be used against you in support of any application by the Official Receiver or the trustee in bankruptcy to suspend your discharge.

If they were sufficiently serious in damaging the interests of the creditors, they could be used to justify the making against you of a bankruptcy restrictions order, or your having to give a bankruptcy restrictions undertaking: see Chapter 22, below.

PART III
HOW BANKRUPTCY ENDS

CHAPTER 22
DISCHARGE

Once you are made bankrupt, by a bankruptcy order against you, or you make yourself bankrupt (see Chapter 6, above), you remain a bankrupt, until:

(1) You are fully discharged under the statute, that is, after the expiry of a fixed time; or
(2) The court makes an order on your application for your discharge; or
(3) The court makes **an order of annulment**, which annuls, that is, cancels, the bankruptcy order against you (see Chapter 23); or
(4) The court makes an order, on your application, for **a re-hearing of the petition**, on new facts coming to light (see Chapter 23), which gives you a second chance of defeating the petition; or
(5) You successfully **appeal to a higher court against the bankruptcy order.**

As explained at page 97, below, discharges, though they occur automatically, or are granted by the court on application, may be suspended (i.e. stopped from operating). You may also have a "Bankruptcy Restrictions Order" made against you, or be made to give a "Bankruptcy Restrictions Undertaking", which handicaps your business activities for the period while it runs: see page 97 below.

DISCHARGES UNDER THE NEW LAW

If you have been made bankrupt after the date when the new bankruptcy laws took effect, that is, 1ˢᵗ **April 2004**, then in the ordinary way, you will be discharged **at the end of one year from the date of the bankruptcy order.** If the Official Receiver, before the end of that year, files with the court a notice that the investigation of your affairs as a bankrupt is not necessary, or has been finished, you will be discharged earlier, as from the date of the filing of that notice. A copy of the Official Receiver's notice is printed in the Appendix at page 197, below.

These discharges are automatic, and need no application by you. You can apply to the court for a **Certificate of Discharge**, for which the court fee is £60.

DISCHARGES UNDER THE OLD LAW (FIRST TIME BANKRUPTCY)

If you were made bankrupt, or made yourself bankrupt, for the first time before that date, i.e. under the old statutes, you will have been automatically discharged, either:

(1) At the end of one year after the date; or
(2) At the end of the period of discharge under the old bankruptcy statutes, if that date was earlier. Those periods were, for ordinary bankruptcy orders (then called "orders of adjudication"), **three years after the bankruptcy order**, or, if you made yourself bankrupt, **two years after that date.**

Different rules apply to people who have had special orders made against them.

DISCHARGE: BANKRUPTCIES UNDER THE OLD LAW (TWO OR MORE TIMES BANKRUPT)

If you were made bankrupt during the **15 YEARS BEFORE 1ˢᵗ APRIL 2004,** that is to say, **AFTER 1ˢᵗ APRIL 1989,** and were then made bankrupt again before **1ˢᵗ APRIL 2004,** you will be automatically discharged at the end of **FIVE YEARS** after 1ˢᵗ APRIL 2004, that is to say, on **1ˢᵗ APRIL 2009.** But you could apply to the court for an earlier date of discharge, if you could show a good case for a shorter period, e.g. that you had been behaving specially well, or had successfully fulfilled any conditions which had been imposed on you by the court.

SUSPENDING THE AUTOMATIC DISCHARGE FOR MISCONDUCT

You will normally be discharged at the end of the first year after your bankruptcy order. But if you have not been doing what the Official Receiver, or your trustee in bankruptcy, or the court have been asking or ordering you to do, for clearing up your affairs, e.g. by explaining your transactions, by helping to get in your property, or by helping to sort out your creditors, the Official Receiver or the trustee in bankruptcy may apply to the court for **an order of suspension** of your discharge.

If the court is satisfied that you have not done, or are not doing, your duty to the Official Receiver, or to the trustee in bankruptcy, or to the court, it may make an order delaying your discharge until a later date, or until you have done what is required of you, or until other conditions have been satisfied.

BANKRUPTCY RESTRICTION ORDERS AND UNDERTAKINGS

Where the court considers you to have behaved very badly, from the point of view of your creditors, in a number of specified ways, the court now has special powers to impose on you what is called a **bankruptcy restrictions order,** or instead to require you to give to the Secretary of State for Trade and Industry what is called a **bankruptcy restrictions undertaking.** These are like the disqualification orders and undertakings which can be made against, or compulsorily given by, directors of companies in winding-up, who have behaved badly, in the same sort of way, in running their companies. A list of the cases of bad behaviour which can lead to such orders is printed in the Appendix at page 204, below.

An application for such an order or an invitation to give such an undertaking can only be made by the Secretary of State for Trade and Industry, or by the Official Receiver at his (or her) direction; it must be made to the court **WITHIN ONE YEAR AFTER THE DATE OF THE BANKRUPTCY ORDER.** It must run for at least TWO YEARS, but cannot run for more than FIFTEEN YEARS.

DEBTS WHICH ARE NOT RELEASED BY A DISCHARGE

The debts from which a bankrupt is not released by a discharge, whether an automatic discharge, or a discharge by order of the court (unless that order otherwise specially provides), are the following:

(1) A fine imposed by a court by way of punishment for an offence;
(2) (a) An obligation (that is, a debt) arising in any family proceeding in court, including a judgment for payment of a lump sum, and an order for the payment of the costs of obtaining that judgment, or
(2) (b) Any obligation (that is, a debt) arising under a maintenance assessment made under the Child Support Act 1991;
Note: Although judgments for a lump sum and for costs are not released by discharge, they have recently been made provable as debts and receive a dividend in the bankruptcy. The party who is liable to pay them is therefore liable, after his discharge, to pay the balance of what remains unpaid of those debts, after what has been paid off them in the bankruptcy.
(3) Any obligation (that is, a debt) arising under a "confiscation order", made by a court under the drug-trafficking laws or the Proceeds of Crime Act 2002;
(4) Debts incurred by the bankrupt, in respect of, or where forbearance in respect of those debts was obtained by, any fraud or fraudulent breach of trust by the bankrupt;
(5) A liability to pay damages for personal injury to any person arising from negligence, nuisance or breach of duty under a contract or a statute or otherwise, or to pay damages under the Consumer Protection Act 1987, except to such extent and on such conditions as the court shall direct;
(6) Debts arising under students' loans, made under the Higher Education Act 2004, subject to the date when the loan was made.

CHAPTER 23
ANNULMENT OF THE BANKRUPTCY ORDER

You are entitled to apply to the court to annul the bankruptcy order against you, at any time, even after you have obtained your discharge. But the court can only grant you an **order of annulment**, if you can comply with some strict conditions. An order of annulment wipes the whole bankruptcy away, but does not affect what has already been done by the trustee in bankruptcy in realising your property and paying your debts. It does not protect you from prosecution for criminal offences (see Chapter 16); but proceedings cannot be started against you after an order of annulment has been made.

The court also has a power to "rescind" its orders, that is, to set them aside, by an order of rescission: see page 104, below.

ANNULMENT ON BANKRUPT'S APPLICATION

There are two forms of annulment for which you can apply;

(a) an application on the ground that, on any grounds that existed at the time when the bankruptcy order was made, it should not have been made; or

(b) an application on the ground that all the debts in your bankruptcy, and interest payable thereon (if due), and all the costs and expenses of the bankruptcy, have been paid in full, or have been covered by security to the satisfaction of the court.

(a) Application on the grounds that the order should not have been made

In this form of application, the court looks at what evidence was before the court on the original hearing of the petition. If it has since been discovered that the petition debt had already been paid, or was illegal, or could not be enforced by the petitioning creditor, or if the judgment on which the debt was based was a default judgment which has been set aside, or, if it was a judgment after trial, it has been set aside on appeal, the bankruptcy order must be annulled.

Procedure

Your application must be supported by witness statements, verified by statements of truth or affidavits, (see page 32 above) in which you, and any other available witnesses, state all the facts necessary to prove your right to an order of annulment.

You must give the Official Receiver, the trustee in bankruptcy and the petitioning creditor **sufficient notice of the hearing of your application** to enable them to attend. The trustee in bankruptcy will generally take no part in the hearing; but he will be concerned as to what orders the court may make, after the order of annulment, to restore you to your ownership and possession of such of your property as has not yet been realised and distributed to your creditors or otherwise applied for the purposes of the bankruptcy.

If parts of your property are in the process of being sold or disposed of at the time when you are making your application, you can apply to the court for an order that any further sales or disposals be suspended until after the hearing. If the trustee in bankruptcy does appear at the hearing, the court will usually order that his costs be paid by the petitioning creditor.

The trustee and the Official Receiver may attend the hearing. The dispute is substantially between yourself and the petitioning creditor.

Cancellation of the bankruptcy entries

If you do obtain an order of annulment on this ground, you need to apply for the registration of your bankruptcy order in the official registers to be cancelled. You can ask for the annulment to be advertised by the Secretary of State for Trade and Industry, in the London Gazette and in the newspaper where your bankruptcy was first advertised, at no cost to you.

(b) "Application on the grounds of payment in full"

This form of application is more complicated and more difficult for obtaining an order of annulment. The court must be satisfied that all of your actual creditors have been paid in full, not merely those who have "proved", that is, made a claim, in your bankruptcy. Interest on proved debts has to be paid, but only out of any surplus arising from the realisation of your property, after all debts have been paid in full; as to interest, see below. All the remuneration of the trustee, and all his expenses and costs, must also be paid or provided for. If that remuneration and those costs and expenses seem exorbitant, you can apply to the court to review them, if any reductions made by the court would assist the payment off of your debts, or would contribute to a surplus of assets to which you would be entitled.

If there are known to be creditors who have not yet proved their debts, the court may direct the trustee in bankruptcy to send them notice of your application, giving them **21 days in which to put in a proof**; it may also require him to advertise your application. It may adjourn your application while this procedure is carried out.

It is only bankruptcy debts which have to be paid, not the debts which cannot be proved in your bankruptcy, but for which you remain liable. As to what debts can and cannot be proved in your bankruptcy, see Chapter 22, above.

The trustee must attend the hearing; the Official Receiver may attend, and must attend if, there being no trustee in bankruptcy, or the trustee has been released, he has put in a report himself. If the court makes an order, it must send a sealed copy to you, to the Official Receiver and to the trustee in bankruptcy.

Third party money: interest on proved debts

It sometimes happens that the property of a bankrupt, when realised, produces enough to pay off the whole bankruptcy, including interest on proved debts. Any surplus resulting comes back to you, unless it has been claimed by a post-bankruptcy creditor, or by a creditor with a non-provable debt.

In the great majority of annulments on the grounds of payment in full, they are paid off out of third party money. In that case, the third party may be required to satisfy the trustee in bankruptcy and the court that it is his own money, and not funds he has been secreting on your behalf.

Where the third party money is being used for the annulment, the court may in addition require the payment of interest out of it, as well as the interest chargeable on the original debts.

Procedure

In this form of application, you must send the Official Receiver and the trustee in bankruptcy **28 days' notice of the hearing of your application;** but you need not give notice to the petitioning creditor.

Your application must be supported by witness statements, verified by statements of truth, or affidavits, which set out all the necessary facts and figures as to your debts and their payment with interest, and the payment of the expenses.

If you think that the fees, costs and expenses claimed by the trustee in bankruptcy are too high, you can ask the court to look at them, with a view to reduction.

The trustee in bankruptcy's report

The trustee in bankruptcy must file in court, **not less than 21 days before the hearing,** a report, of which he must send you a copy **not less than 14 days before the hearing.** His report will deal with circumstances leading up to the bankruptcy, a summary of your property and liabilities, at the date of the bankruptcy order and at the date of the application, with the names and addresses of known creditors who have not proved their debts.

He must also report any other matters about which he thinks it right to inform the court, such as how you have behaved with reference to your creditors before the bankruptcy, and how you have behaved to him and to the Official Receiver during the bankruptcy.

Important things which he will report will be whether you have done any transactions at an undervalue, or by way of preference; see Chapter 20, above.

If there is no outside trustee in bankruptcy, the Official Receiver will make the report. The Official Receiver can in any event submit his own report to the court, sending you a copy **not less than 7 days before the hearing.**

You can reply to or contradict statements in the reports with which you disagree, or add further evidence in the form of a witness statement, in support of your application; you must send copies of your comments or your further evidence to the Official Receiver and the trustee in bankruptcy.

The court has a discretion to grant or withhold orders of annulment

You may be able to effect the total payment-off of all the debts, with interest (if due) and expenses, in your bankruptcy; but you will not necessarily thereby obtain your order of annulment from the court. The court has a discretion to grant or refuse an order, dependent on the circumstances of the bankruptcy. Sometimes the court considers that the bankruptcy is too old to be annulled, because the court's records, or the creditors' accounts, may have been shredded.

Cancellation of bankruptcy entries

See page 100, above.

ANNULMENT ON OTHER GROUNDS

The court will also order an annulment, in the course of other procedures.

On the approval of an individual voluntary arrangement (see Chapter 24, below), the court will annul the bankruptcy order, on your application, or, if you do not apply, on the application of the Official Receiver.

On the approval of a "fast-track voluntary arrangement" (see Chapter 24, below), the court will annul the bankruptcy order on the application of the Official Receiver.

RESCISSION OF BANKRUPTCY ORDER

The court has a general power to set aside its orders, for good reasons. This includes the power to "rescind", that is, to set aside, a bankruptcy order, where there has been a change of circumstances. But in principle this power can only be appealed to by the creditors, e.g. where they have come to think that they will not do as well out of the realisation of your property, if you remain bankrupt, as if you cease to be one.

Debt Management or Arrangement Companies

There are now a large number of companies who offer to carry out, for people in financial difficulty for a fee, advisory or company voluntary arrangements. If you decide to employ one of these you should take great care to check its bona fides, legal standing, and efficiency, and to ask for references, as there are some companies in this field who behave badly and/or inefficiently and/or charge extortionate fees.

The Government is introducing a Bill into parliament which, among other thing, will enable people who promote Debt Management Schemes and Debt Repayment Plans to be controlled: see Chapter 43, Page 179, below.

PART IV
ALTERNATIVES TO BANKRUPTCY

CHAPTER 24

INDIVIDUAL VOLUNTARY ARRANGEMENTS AND DEEDS OF ARRANGEMENT

There are at present three alternatives to bankruptcy as a solution to personal indebtedness. These are:

(a) the ordinary individual voluntary arrangement;
(b) the "Fast track" individual arrangement ("FTIVA");
(c) the deed of arrangement.

Cheaper and easier procedures for individual voluntary arrangement cases are in the process of being worked out by the Government.

Additional procedures are also being prepared by the Government, particularly designed for "consumer debtors", and largely for non-business debt cases. But these will not be available for some time: see Chapter 43, page 179 below.

(A) THE INDIVIDUAL VOLUNTARY ARRANGEMENT

The individual voluntary arrangement (often abbreviated to "I V A"), is a procedure for getting your creditors to meet together legally on a formal basis, and for putting before them your proposals for an agreement with them, and between them, for the collection and sharing out of your assets among them, and/or for your making of contributions to them from your future earnings or business profits.

This procedure can be used both before you are made bankrupt, and after. It is available in two forms:

1. the normal arrangement, proposed by a debtor in difficulties, or
   by an undischarged bankrupt, which must be administered by
   an insolvency practitioner, or someone equally qualified, and
2. the so-called "fast-track voluntary arrangement", which is con-
   fined to undischarged bankrupts, and must be administered by
   the Official Receiver: see below.

(1) THE NORMAL FORM OF VOLUNTARY ARRANGEMENT

Your creditors are officially summoned by the "nominee" who will be chairman (see page 110) to a formal meeting, to consider your proposals, first your original ones, or as they have been modified with your consent. If they agree by the necessary majority to approve them, then this amounts to an agreement which is binding between you and your creditors, and between all your creditors who had notice of the meeting, whether they attended it and voted on the proposals or not.

Any bankruptcy proceedings on foot against you are then dismissed, and you are saved from all the difficulties, dangers and disqualifications of bankruptcy.

The difficulties with the normal arrangement

There are however difficulties and problems for the small debtor in the normal voluntary arrangements procedure. First, you cannot organise and run it by yourself; it has to be set up and managed, and the meeting of creditors has to be summoned and conducted, by a licensed insolvency practitioner (see Chapter 17, page 67 above), or by an insolvency specialist having similar qualifications for dealing with bankruptcy cases.

This means that you cannot effectively be a litigant in person for this procedure.

Secondly, the procedure is under the control of the court, which normally has to make an "interim order" (see below). It will not make the order, unless it is satisfied with your bona fides, and with the serious character of your proposals, and of the reasonable prospects of your proposals being approved by your creditors, and of succeeding in their stated objectives.

Thirdly, the practitioner's fees and expenses are quite high, and a good deal of money is needed up front to obtain their commitment; they can amount to £10,000.

Fourthly, you have to convince the practitioner of the correctness, soundness and good faith of your proposals, in which he himself has to state his own belief.

Since this form of arrangement must be set up and carried into effect by a practitioner, only the outlines of the procedure are given below, to help you to understand what is going on.

The procedure

The procedure is for you, with the assistance of the practitioner (who from this stage on is called "the nominee"), to prepare "proposals", to be placed before the creditors. You have to be absolutely frank with him, and entirely honest about all the property you own, and all your debts and liabilities, including the contingent and prospective ones.

You have to prepare for him a statement of your affairs. You must be equally frank and honest, and not fanciful, in your statements to him about your future prospects, if relevant to your proposals. As stated above, he has to confirm his own belief that the proposals have a reasonable prospect of being approved at a meeting of creditors, and of being carried into effect.

You have to be very sure that you have included the names, addresses and claims of all your creditors, even if you dislike them, or don't believe in the genuineness of their claims. If a genuine creditor is not included and served with notice to attend the meeting, he may not be bound by the result, and has the right to complain at the result.

The interim order

While the proposals are being prepared by the nominee, application must usually be made by your or on your behalf to the correct county court (the one where you would be made bankrupt), for an **"interim order"**. Your application has to be supported by witness statements, verifying the proposals, and stating many other details.

The interim order acts as a moratorium, to keep creditors off your back during the arrangement procedure. Once that order is made, it becomes almost impossible for any of your creditors to take proceedings against you, or to start or continue with a bankruptcy petition, or to levy execution or distress against your house or property. This protection continues in force until your proposals are accepted by the creditors or rejected.

You are not obliged to apply for an interim order, if you are advised that it is not necessary.

Acceptance of your proposals

If your proposals are accepted by the necessary majority, the nominee is re-named "the supervisor". He then administers the arrangement, like a trustee in bankruptcy, in accordance with the agreed proposals. If your proposals do not succeed in producing the promised results, the supervisor may terminate the arrangement. The necessary majority is in principle 75%, but there are special rules affecting the voting rights.

If you seriously misconduct yourself with the supervisor, by misleading him, or not doing what your proposals promised, or by not providing him with the assistance which he requires from you to make it succeed, he is entitled, and may be legally obliged, to present a bankruptcy petition against you himself. If he thinks that you may have committed offences, he must report them to the prosecution authorities.

(2) THE FAST-TRACK VOLUNTARY ARRANGEMENT

You can only use this procedure, after you have been made bankrupt and are still undischarged.

As an undischarged bankrupt, you can submit to the Official Receiver a voluntary arrangement which you wish to propose to your creditors, together with a statement of your affairs, with full details of your property and your creditors, and of your preferential creditors, and how they are to be dealt with (they have to be paid ahead of all other creditors). The proposal must also show that the Official Receiver is to be the nominee for the purposes of the arrangement.

It must also show how any of your creditors who are your "associates" (see Chapter 21, above) are to be dealt with, and whether claims have been made, or are likely to be made, to set aside any of your transactions as having been made at an undervalue, or by way of preference (see Chapter 21, above), or as having been of an extortionate nature, that is to say, where an excessive amount of interest has been charged.

Action by the Official Receiver

Within 28 days of receiving your application, the Official Receiver must send you a notice, stating either:

(a) that he agrees to act as nominee of your proposed arrangement, or
(b) that he refuses to act as nominee, giving his reasons, or
(c) that with the information with which he has been supplied, he cannot reach a decision, and stating what further information he requires. The basis for the Official Receiver agreeing or refusing to act is whether the proposal has a reasonable prospect of being approved by the creditors.

If the Official Receiver states that he needs further information, and you supply it, he must reply further **within 28 days of receiving it.** He must state whether he accepts or refuses to act as nominee, or wants still further information.

If he does agree to act, you must pay him a fee of £335 for his services in so acting.

Action when the Official Receiver agrees to act as nominee

If the Official Receiver agrees to act as nominee of the arrangement, he must, as soon as reasonably practicable, send to your creditors, that is, the creditors in the bankruptcy, whose claims and whose addresses he knows, and to the trustee in bankruptcy (if not himself), a copy of your proposal, and a notice inviting the creditors to vote, either approving or rejecting it. His notice to creditors must explain how he will decide whether the creditors have approved or rejected it. He must not invite them to suggest any modifications of the arrangement. There is, with this form of arrangement, no actual meeting of creditors, and therefore no formal discussion between them.

If three-quarters of the creditors who vote approve the proposal, the Official Receiver must, as soon as reasonably practicable, report to the court that the proposal has been approved. When he makes that report, the arrangement starts to bind you and all the creditors who were entitled to vote on it. There are provisions protecting the rights of creditors who were not informed of the proposal.

The Official Receiver acts as supervisor of the arrangement, and will charge a fee of 15% (collected out of the realisations).

The Official Receiver must apply to the court to annul your bankruptcy order; but he must not apply until after 28 days from making his report to the court, to allow any persons entitled to challenge the approval to do so.

Advantages of fast-track voluntary arrangement

This form of arrangement with your creditors does not require the services of an expensive practitioner; the only official charge is the £335 fee to the Official Receiver, for which he must do the writing to the creditors, and his fee to administer the arrangement if approved; that fee and his expenses are paid out of the realisation of your property. There is also no meeting, at which hostile creditors could sway the vote against you.

The disadvantage is that the Official Receiver has the sole right to decide whether to act or not. His decision depends on the structure and credibility of your proposal.

(B) THE DEED OF ARRANGEMENT

You can enter into a deed of arrangement with your creditors under the Deeds of Arrangement Act 1914 (as amended). This is a less complicated, and less expensive, procedure than the individual voluntary arrangement; but it must equally be carried out by a qualified insolvency practitioner, as trustee, who will normally charge a substantial up-front fee. He prepares your proposal, in the form of a deed (a formal legal document), and summons a meeting of your creditors to consider it.

If a majority of your creditors who attend the meeting agree to your proposal, some of them will sign the deed; the trustee will then register it. But the deed does not become binding on you or on any of your creditors, until **a majority of your creditors, in number and in value** (not just those who attended the meeting) have assented to it in writing (with a witness) (that is, agreed to the deed). The trustee must, **within 28 days after the registration of the deed, file with the Deeds** of Arrangement Registry a statutory declaration, stating that the necessary number of assents has been obtained.

The trustee is paid a percentage of the value of his recoveries, as laid down in the deed.

PART V
LEGAL AID AND ADVICE

CHAPTER 25
LEGAL AID AND ADVICE : SOURCES OF HELP

This book has been planned and written to help people who are involved in bankruptcy or winding-up proceedings, or who are likely to become involved in such proceedings in court, and who cannot afford the costs of instructing lawyers to advise them and to appear in court on their behalf. Since they are legally entitled to appear in court in person to conduct their case, this book is intended to help them to do that.

But it may be that you feel unable to embark on the conducting of your court case in person, or that having started your case in person, it has become too difficult for you to continue. You will need to know what sources of help are available to you, to which you can apply to obtain either legal advice or legal representation in court by a barrister or a solicitor. These sources of help are made available by the Government, and by charitable and other bodies.

There is a problem about legal aid, described below, whether administered by the Legal Services Commission, the Law Centres or the Citizens Advice Bureaux. Legal representation in court is not available for cases which involve the running of a business. If you have been running a business, therefore, you apparently can't get legal aid from any body which is financed by the Legal Services Commission.

But after you have been made bankrupt, you might be able to get legal help or representation in proceedings brought by your trustee in bankruptcy against you or your family, or by yourself or members of your family, relating to the family home: see Chapter 20 above. It is however likely to be withheld if the applicant will not "benefit" from the proceedings; this raises the question of what is the benefit attributable to the defence of a bankruptcy petition.

The Legal Services Commission

This is a Government body, coming under the Department for Constitutional Affairs; it replaced the former Legal Aid Board. Its job is to supply what are now called "community-funded legal services", the new name for legal aid. These services come in two forms, a certificate for legal representation in court, and the grant of "Legal Help", which is for giving legal advice, replacing the former "Green Card" legal advice service.

The Commission publishes a very useful "Practical Guide to Community Legal Service Funding", which is obtainable free, on application by phone.

The Commission does not do much providing of legal services itself. It makes contracts for the supply of these with solicitors, with firms, and such bodies as the Law Centres and the Citizens Advice Bureaux. Any firm or body with which it enters into a contract has to possess a quality mark certificate as to its efficiency.

In addition to the rule about not assisting in cases involving the running of a business, referred to above, the Commission imposes strict conditions on applicants to qualify for legal assistance. For legal representation, there is a stiff means test; applicants with more than modest amounts of savings will not qualify. There are also provisions for requiring the making of contributions out of income or capital.

The Commission's postal address, website address and e-mail address are printed in the Appendix at page 206, below, and the addresses of its Regional Offices are printed at page 209, below.

The Insolvency Service

This is the Government body which regulates bankruptcy, insolvency and winding-up, and employs the Official Receivers who do that work; it comes under the Department for Trade and Industry. It has a website, and also an "insolvency helpline" website for giving advice to the public, including advice by telephone. Changes in the law are posted on the main website: those addresses are also printed in the Appendix at page 206.

The Law Centres

The Law Centre is a charitable company, limited by guarantee, and financed largely by the Legal Services Commission, and also partly by local authorities and other funds. The Centre gives legal advice generally, and also "Legal Help" for the Law Commission, and to a limited extent conducts cases in court for its clients. There is also a service called "Help at Court", where a very limited involvement of a lawyer is required. The Centre is, of course, bound by the Commission's conditions and means tests, in cases where it acts for the Commission. All Centres belong to the Law Centres Federation.

The qualifications for obtaining "Legal Help" or "Help at Court" from the Commission or its contracted suppliers are the same as for full legal representation, described above.

There are currently 64 Centres in England, Wales and Northern Ireland, not very evenly distributed. There are also centres in Scotland, where the laws are different. A list of the Law Centres with the addresses is printed in the Appendix at page 211.

The Citizens Advice Bureaux

The Citizens Advice Bureau is an advice centre organised by a charitable body, called "Citizens Advice", at approximately 3,500 addresses. Some Bureaux also enter into contracts with the Commission to supply legal assistance.

For the qualifications for obtaining "Legal Help", see above under "Law Centres".

The addresses of their headquarters are printed in the Appendix at page 207, below. The addresses of their local bureaux will be found in the telephone directory, and can also be looked up on their website.

The Bar Pro Bono Unit

This is a charitable organisation run by barristers, which provides, in suitable cases, legal representation in court by a barrister. Its conditions for taking on a case are:

That the case has legal merit, that the applicant cannot get public legal funding, and has no other source of assistance (such as under an insurance policy or from a trade union), that the services of a Pro Bono barrister are needed, and that no other way is available to cope with the case. An applicant should, if possible, have already had advice from a solicitor, who might be willing to continue to act in the case with the barrister.

The addresses of its office and of its website are printed in the Appendix at page 208, below.

The Solicitors Pro Bono Group

This charitable organisation seeks to match up solicitors' firms with organisations offering legal advice.

The address of its website is printed in the Appendix at page 208, below.

The Royal Courts of Justice Advice Desk

For people living or working in London, and facing, or involved in, bankruptcy proceedings in the Bankruptcy Court at the High Court, there is a Royal Courts of Justice advice Bureau, located in the Royal Courts of Justice, in the Strand, which maintains a "Bankruptcy Court Advice Desk". This gives free, independent and confidential legal advice on all aspects of bankruptcy; it may also be able to provide free legal representation to defend bankruptcy petitions, or in other bankruptcy proceedings:

For fuller details, see Appendix, Part 3, page 206, below.

The Bankruptcy Advisory Service

This is a private organisation, which invites subscriptions for the use of its advisory service in cases of debt and bankruptcy, including negotiations with creditors, and the protection of the matrimonial home.

Its address is printed in the Appendix at page 208, below.

There are other Advice Centres throughout the country, which may be able to give you useful legal advice; but they are unlikely to be able to provide legal representation.

PART VI
WINDING UP OF COMPANIES AND PARTNERSHIPS

CHAPTER 26

WHAT IS A COMPANY? HOW DOES IT WORK?

A limited company is called "limited", because the liabilities of the people who run it to pay its debts, if it cannot do so out of its own resources, are in general "limited" to the money which they have "invested", that is, put into it, in buying the shares, or in providing the company with some of its pieces of property in exchange for shares. Large companies are now called "PLC", which means "public limited company", as distinct from the small company, which is still called "Ltd". The PLC is regulated by different laws and rules to the "Ltd" company.

OTHER LIABILITIES

Despite those basic limitations of liability for the people who run a limited company (from now on referred to as "a company" or "the company"), they may still be held personally liable to its creditors for more than the amount of their investment in the company, if they have run it badly, negligently or fraudulently (see Chapters 38 to 39, below).

HOW A COMPANY COMES INTO BEING

A company begins its life when the people who are forming it, that is, setting it up, register it at a Government office called Companies House. The company must have its own constitution and rules (called "the memorandum and articles"), which legally lay down what sort of business, or businesses, it is being set up to do, what is to be the amount of its "capital", that is, the value, number and types of its shares, and how it must behave to the Government, its officers, its shareholders and its creditors.

A company has to have a "registered office", which is its legal address, at or to which legal papers can be validly delivered or posted, or in some cases sent by fax or e-mail. The registered office can be at the company's principal place of business, but is most frequently nowadays located at the office of its solicitors, auditors or accountants.

A COMPANY IS A LEGAL PERSON

A company is in law a legal person, which can own property, carry on business, do illegal or criminal things, be prosecuted and fined, and, at the end of its commercial life, dies by being dissolved. It does not die just by being wound up. A company acts by means of the actions of those who control it, that is, its directors, managers, or other persons who are authorised to act on its behalf. In general, a company is liable for all the acts or omissions of those who run it, and who are authorised to do such things.

THE PROPERTY OF THE COMPANY

The property which the company buys, earns by carrying on its business, or acquires by other means, and with which, or by means of which, it carries on its business, including generally the premises where it carries on that business, belongs to it as completely as your own property belongs to you.

That property never belongs to the people who run it, nor to its shareholders, except:

(1) when the company has been or is being wound-up. At that stage, the shareholders are entitled to share out whatever property is left, after all the debts and expenses have been paid;
(2) if the company gets the permission of the court to return some of its capital to its shareholders, that is, to buy back its shares.

A company must not make presents to its directors, officers or shareholders, except as permitted by its constitution or by the law, or as authorised by a shareholders' meeting. It can only lend money to any of them under very strict conditions. It must not make such presents, by means of selling or transferring to them pieces of its property for less than their real value. If its directors or officers or shareholders have lent it money, it must not repay that money to them in a way which, if it is insolvent and unable to pay all creditors equally, would prefer the person it is paying to its other creditors (see Chapter 38, below).

CHAPTER 27
INSOLVENT PARTNERSHIPS

A partnership is a group consisting of members called "partners", that is individual persons, companies or partnerships, who have entered into a partnership agreement to carry on business together. For the purposes of that business, unlike limited companies, they are subject to unlimited personal liability for the partnership's debts: but see page 126 below. There are special laws and rules which regulate their business life and their winding-up. Partnerships were formerly capable, when insolvent, of being put into bankruptcy, under the old laws, but they now have their own special laws and rules for putting them into winding-up.

For the purposes of a partnership being wound-up when insolvent, it is treated as an unregistered company, and the partners are treated as officers of that company.

Because of its special constitution, a partnership has to be capable of being wound-up in several different ways. This chapter will only describe the two simplest.

Claim by a creditor

A creditor for a sum **exceeding** £750 may serve on the partnership, and on each member of it, a written demand for the debt to be paid either by the partnership, or by a member of it, **within 21 days**, or that the partnership, or its members, shall give security for or compound for the debt within that period. Such a demand may not be made for a future debt (as it can be made against a company or an individual). The form of demand (Form IPO 4), is different from that used for companies.

On non-payment of the debt, or on failure to give security or to compound for the debt, the creditor may present a winding-up petition against the partnership as an unregistered company, together with winding-up petitions against those members which are companies or partnerships, and bankruptcy petitions against those members who are individuals.

Claim by an unpaid member for a partnership debt

Where a member of the partnership has paid, or has had to pay, a debt due by the partnership, and has not been reimbursed by the partnership for his payment, he may serve on the partnership a written demand for that sum in the same manner as above. If he is not reimbursed, he may present a winding-up petition against the partnership.

The procedure under the petition will be the same as for a company: see Chapters 31 to 33, below. There are special rules regarding the matrimonial homes of individual members, much the same as those applying in bankruptcy: see Chapter 20, above.

Other procedures

An insolvent partnership can, instead of being wound-up, enter into a "partnership voluntary arrangement" with its creditors, if they agree (see Chapter 41, below), or can appoint an administrator for the purpose of going into administration, or have an administrator appointed for that purpose by the court, or by the holder of an agricultural charge into which the partnership has entered (see Chapter 42, below).

Limited liability

Limited liability partnerships, which have limited liability to their creditors, are also subject to special rules, and are wound up as unregistered companies.

Disqualification of officers

Directors, including other officers and "shadow directors", may be disqualified by the court, if found to be unfit to be concerned with the management of a company: see Chapter 35, below.

CHAPTER 28
WINDING-UP A COMPANY: COMPULSORY OR VOLUNTARY

A company can be wound up by its members very simply at any time, while it is solvent and able to pay all its debts in full. This procedure is carried out by a resolution passed at a shareholders' meeting, and need not concern us here.

When a company cannot pay its debts in full as they fall due, it is said to be "insolvent". It must then either be wound-up (or "liquidated" as it is often called), or enter into an arrangement with its creditors, called a "corporate voluntary arrangement" (see Chapter 41, below), or into "administration" (see Chapter 42, below).

"Insolvent winding-up", as it is called, is carried out in two ways, "compulsory winding-up" or "creditors' voluntary winding-up"; these are roughly the equivalent of a person being made bankrupt, or making himself bankrupt (see Chapter 6, above).

(A) "Creditors' voluntary winding-up"

Where you and your fellow-directors of a company, or you and your fellow partners in a partnership, realise, or are advised by your auditors or financial advisers, that the company (or the partnership) cannot pay its debts as they fall due, and is therefore insolvent, you and they must take prompt action. Otherwise, you may all expose yourselves to personal liability to the company's creditors.

If the amount needed to pay the debts can be calculated, and the company has available unissued shares, the company can issue more shares to its directors, or to others who are aware of the company's difficulties, to raise the necessary sum, or it can borrow that sum from them.

Otherwise, you must resolve either (a) to arrange for a creditors' voluntary winding-up to be put in hand, or (b) that the company should present its own winding-up petition to the court, or (c) to go for one of the other procedures, referred to above and in Chapters 41 and 42.

If you resolve to go for creditors' voluntary winding-up, or to use one of those procedures, it will be completely set up for you by your advisers, with an insolvency practitioner acting as liquidator, supervisor or administrator; so they will not be further explained in detail here.

In the case of a creditors' voluntary winding-up, two meetings have to be called, one of the company's creditors, and the other of the company's shareholders.

If the creditors at their meeting do not vote in favour of a creditors' voluntary winding-up, and do not favour either of the other procedures, then the company has to go into compulsory winding-up, by a winding-up petition, presented to the court either by a creditor or by the company itself.

This Part is concerned with explaining the procedure for, and the consequences of, a winding-up petition presented by a creditor, and how, if you wish, you can oppose it. It will also explain what, after a winding-up order is made, are its consequences and what liabilities it creates, for you and your fellow-directors or fellow-partners.

(B) Compulsory winding-up

When

(a) a company is pressed by one or more creditors for an overdue payment of his debt or their debts, and it does not pay the debt or debts, or does not pay in full, or

(b) one of its creditors has obtained judgment against the company, and has "levied execution", (see below) which did not produce enough money to satisfy the debt, the costs of the judgment and the costs of the execution, or

(c) the creditors have not voted in favour of a creditors' voluntary winding-up: see Chapter 27,

a creditor with a debt exceeding £750 is likely to start proceedings for a compulsory winding-up.

"Execution" is a procedure whereby judgment creditors can get a court order to "levy execution" on the premises or goods of the person against whom they have got judgment. This involves High Court enforcement officers, or county court bailiffs, entering the company's or the partnership's premises, and seizing and removing its goods, for sale by auction, to raise an amount sufficient to pay off the amounts of the judgment, and costs, and the costs of the execution (see further, Chapter 4, page 11 above).

Service of proceedings

Proceedings for a compulsory winding-up are usually begun by "serving on" (that is, delivering to), the company, normally at its registered office (see page 124 above), a legal form called "a statutory demand" for the debt due to the creditor, plus any accrued interest. If the debt is a judgment debt, the demand will usually include the amount of any costs ordered to be paid.

If, as is usual nowadays, the company's registered office is at the office of its solicitors, auditors or accountants, it is a good idea to remind them that, if a statutory demand is served on them, they must let the company know, and pass it on to the company, **at once**. The time-limits for dealing with statutory demands are tight.

Where there has been an unsatisfied execution, no statutory demand needs to be served, before serving a winding-up petition: see below.

The procedure by statutory demand

The statutory demand requires the company to pay the amount claimed to be due to the creditor **within 21 days from the date of the service of the document on the company,** or to agree to "secure the debt", or "compound for it" with the creditor within that time.

"Securing for the debt" means giving the creditor a security over some property belonging to the company, or to someone else, and thereby persuading him to accept that in settlement for the debt.

"Compounding for the debt" means getting the creditor to agree to accept a lesser sum than the debt, in full and final settlement.

Where the company has suffered an unsatisfied execution (see above), the creditor need not serve a statutory demand on the company; the failure of the execution to produce enough money to satisfy the execution creditor's debt in full is treated as legal proof that it is insolvent, which can be relied on by any creditor of the company. A winding-up petition can therefore be served on the company straightaway, although a letter will usually be written first by the creditor or his solicitors to warn the company of what is intended.

CHAPTER 29

THE STATUTORY DEMAND: HOW TO DEAL WITH IT

Note: *In this Chapter, and in succeeding Chapters, what is stated about the winding-up of a company is generally applicable also to the winding-up of an insolvent partnership; mention will be made of any differences of procedure: see Chapter 27 above.*

As explained above, a "statutory demand" is a legal Court Form, issued by someone who is a creditor of a company, and served on the company, demanding payment of a sum of money, which is claimed to be owing and currently due for payment to him by the company.

The creditor is also entitled to claim payment from the company of a debt which, though it is not currently due for payment, is due for payment in the future, on a fixed date, if he can satisfy the court that, when it does become due for payment, the company will be unable to pay it. This cannot be claimed against a partnership and is generally not an easy matter to prove.

The statutory demand to be used for the winding-up of a company is similar to, but not exactly the same as, the Court Forms used in the case of a statutory demand issued in bankruptcy. Those Forms of statutory demand are discussed and explained, in relation to bankruptcy, in Chapters 7 and 8, pages 23 and 25, above.

You should read those Chapters, but you should bear in mind the important difference between the two Forms of demand. That difference is as follows.

The difference in the Forms of statutory demand

In the case of the statutory demands used in bankruptcy cases, the individual debtor on whom the demand is served has the right, if he disputes the creditor's claim, to apply to the court, the name and address of which is given in the demand, to set aside the statutory demand.

If he does make that application, the creditor cannot present a bankruptcy petition against him for that debt, until the application has been heard and decided. If he succeeds in his application, the creditor cannot present a petition for the debt at all.

In the case of the statutory demand used in company winding-up cases, the company is given no such right to apply to set aside the demand. But it does have two similar rights, by way of application, to resist it.

The company's rights in dealing with the statutory demand

The first is its right to apply to the court to prevent a winding-up petition being presented against the company at all.

The second of these rights is its right, after it has been served with a winding-up petition, based on its non-compliance with a statutory demand, or on an unsatisfied execution, to apply to the court to prevent the petition being advertised, before it is heard.

Which court to apply to

The court to which the company must apply (whose address is stated in the statutory demand), will usually be the Companies Court, part of the Royal Courts of Justice, Strand, London. The High Court (Chancery Division) also sits in the District Registries of the following major provincial cities and towns: Birmingham, Bristol, Cardiff, Leeds, Liverpool, Manchester, Newcastle-upon-Tyne, and Preston. Those courts have the power to hear winding-up petitions from anywhere in England and Wales.

But where a company's issued capital (that is, its shares), which is paid-up, or credited as paid-up, is not greater than £120,000, a petition to wind it up can also be presented to the county court, within whose district the company's registered office is situated.

Who are the judges?

The judges who sit in the Companies Court and in the District Registries to hear winding-up petitions are called "Registrars"; the judges who sit in the county court to hear winding-up petitions are called "District Judges". Registrars and District Judges must be addressed as "Sir" or "Madam".

But where application is made to the court for an injunction, this must be heard by a judge of a higher grade, in the High Court, by a High Court judge, who is to be addressed as "Your Lordship", or "Your Ladyship" and in the county court, by a county court judge, who is to be addressed as "Your Honour".

What the creditor has to do in presenting and advertising the winding-up petition

After the period of 21 days allowed by the statutory demand (or any longer period allowed by the court: see below) for payment of the debt has expired, without the company making payment in full, or securing or compounding for the debt, or otherwise settling with the company, the creditor is entitled to present a winding-up petition based on that non-payment.

After the creditor has presented the petition, he must (a) no sooner than seven days after the date of the service of the petition on the company, and (b) no later than seven days before the date fixed for its hearing, advertise the petition once in the London Gazette (an official publication), or (sometimes) in a newspaper. Such advertisement is, of course, very damaging to the company's credit and business dealings, and should not be allowed to happen, unless the debt on which the petition is based can be properly established and proved. You should note the short times allowed for the advertisement.

Contents of the statutory demand

Full particulars of the debt claimed must be given on page 2 of the statutory demand. These include (i) the date when the debt was incurred, and (ii) for what "consideration" it was incurred, that is, what did the company get, or what was it to get in exchange for the money it was liable to pay, or on whatever other basis the company is alleged to have become indebted to the creditor.

Particulars must also be given of any sums claimed by way of interest or costs, and of any other charges which are claimed by the creditor to have attached to the debt.

Security held by the creditor for the debt demanded

If the creditor holds any security for the debt over any piece of property belonging to the company, full particulars of this must be stated on page 3 of the demand, with its estimated value in money. The amount of this estimated value, when deducted from the debt claimed, must leave a balance due **amounting to at least £751.**

Security for the debt owed by the company, which is held by the creditor over the property of persons other than the company, does not have to be stated, nor does its value have to be taken into consideration in calculating the balance of the debt.

The creditor's estimate of the value of his security can be disputed by the company.

Dealing with the statutory demand by payment

The statutory demand requires payment of the amount claimed **within 21 days of the date when the demand was served on the company.** This period can however be extended by means of an application to the court; this application can be made both before the period expires or after it has expired.

How to apply to the court to extend time to pay

Application must be made to the court on an "originating application", Court Form Form 7.1; a form is printed in the Appendix, at page 193, below. In the High Court, application is made to the Court Manager; in the county court, it is made to the District Judge. The application must be supported by a witness statement, verified by a statement of truth (see Chapter 9, at page 32, above). Good reasons must be given to justify any extension, especially after the period has expired. The court officials will tell you the court fee for the application.

Other ways of complying with the statutory demand

The statutory demand invites the company, if unable to pay the debt in full, "to secure for it" or "to compound for it".

"Securing for the debt" means giving the creditor a security for his debt over property of the company, or of some other person, and obtaining his agreement to accept it in payment of the debt.

"Compounding for the debt" means getting the creditor to agree to accept a lesser sum than his full debt, in full and final settlement, either as a lump sum or by fixed instalments.

Where the company has suffered an "unsatisfied execution"

Where an execution has been levied on the company's property, which was "unsatisfied", that is, it did not produce enough money to pay off the whole sum for which the execution was levied (see Chapter 28, at page 129, above), the creditor need not serve a statutory demand on the company, before presenting a winding-up petition against it.

The fact that the company has been found to have insufficient property to satisfy the execution is treated by the court as proof that it is insolvent and unable to pay its debts, to the same effect as non-payment of the statutory demand.

The creditor is therefore entitled to present a winding-up petition, based on the company's insolvency, straightaway. The debt for which execution was levied does not need to have been his own debt.

Although the creditor does not need to serve a statutory demand, the company still has the right to apply to the court to prevent the advertisement of the petition; but the fact of an execution against the company having remained unsatisfied will present difficulties in getting the court to agree to this.

The creditor is not required to serve a statutory demand before presenting his petition, but he, or his solicitors, will normally write to the company before doing so.

What the company must do, if it cannot settle the statutory demand

If the company has been unable to pay the creditor, or otherwise to settle with him, as an alternative to winding-up, it must apply for an injunction: see Chapter 30, below.

CHAPTER 30

HOW THE COMPANY OR THE PARTNERSHIP APPLIES FOR INJUNCTIONS

Although, as explained above, the company is not entitled to apply to the court to set the statutory demand aside, it is entitled to apply to the court for injunctions, either to prevent the presentation of the petition, or to prevent its advertisement. If the company's first application is successful, it has more or less the same effect as an order setting aside the demand; success in the second application protects the company from the immediate harmful effect of the advertisement on its business and credit.

The company can apply for two sorts of injunction:

(1) an injunction preventing the creditor from presenting a petition, on the ground of the non-payment of the statutory demand, or on the basis of the unsatisfied execution, and

(2) an injunction preventing the creditor from advertising a petition, which he has presented, on the ground that there is no debt due from the company, and that the presentation of the petition would be "an abuse of process".

The company is entitled to apply for such injunctions, if it can put forward in evidence good grounds for objecting to paying the debt demanded. Such grounds may be one or more of the following:

(a) the debt is not owed by the company at all; or

(b) it is not owed in a sum exceeding £750, or

(c) it is not a legal debt, or

(d) it can no longer be claimed against the company, because it is barred by "limitation", that is, the debt is too old to be enforced (as to this ground, see below, page 138), or

(e) the creditor holds security for his debt over a piece of the company's property, the estimated value of which, when deducted from the amount claimed, would leave a sum owing of less than £751; or

(f) the company is entitled to a counterclaim, set-off or cross-demand against the creditor, which is for an equal or a larger sum of money than the sum claimed by the creditor; or

(g) the company has made an agreement with the creditor to secure the debt, or to compound for it (see Chapter 29, above), or to pay it off by instalments.

In addition to possible grounds such as the foregoing, for objecting that the debt is not due, or is not claimable, there may exist, or may have existed, other special factors, such as that the debt is illegal or founded on an illegal contract, other special circumstances forming part of the business relationships between the company and the creditor, which may invalidate the creditor's claim; details of any of these grounds should be stated.

Limitation

Under statutes called "the Limitation Acts", debts and other sums of money cannot generally be recovered by legal proceedings, where six years have passed, since the debt or sum of money first became due to the creditor, or, where it is in the form of a judgment or order of a court, and twelve years have passed, without legal proceedings having been started, unless, during those periods of six years or of twelve years, the company liable to pay it has in some positive way admitted to the creditor that the debt or sum of money is due.

Time periods for the company applying for an injunction

An application for **the first sort of injunction,** to prevent the presentation of a petition, if it is to be effective, must be made to the court, and an order of the court must be obtained, **before the period of 21 days after the service of the demand, which is allowed for payment, has expired.**

If the petition has already been presented and served on the company, an application **for the second sort of injunction,** to prevent it being advertised, if it is to be effective, must be made to the court, and an order of the court must be obtained, **before the period of seven days**

after service has expired, when the creditor is legally bound to advertise the petition.

Applying for the creditor's consent to stop presentation or advertisement of the petition

The time limits for effectively obtaining either sort of injunction are very tight. The company should therefore try to obtain the creditor's consent to hold up its presentation or advertisement, until the company's "with notice" application for an injunction can be heard by the court.

If the company on receiving the statutory demand wishes to dispute it, and stop the presentation of a winding-up petition, or if it has been served with the petition, and wishes to stop its advertisement, it should at once telephone the creditor's solicitors to ask them to agree, if they have not yet presented the petition, to hold it up until after the hearing, or if they have presented it but not yet advertised it, to hold up advertisement until after the hearing.

It would be useful if the person who speaks to them will be appointed to be the company's representative to appear in court on the hearings. Whoever speaks to the solicitors should make a careful note of the time of the call, who was spoken to, and what they said.

If the solicitors refuse consent

If the solicitors refuse to agree to hold up presentation of the petition, or its advertisement, or say that they cannot get instructions from the creditor, they should be told that the company will immediately make a "without notice" application to the court for an "interim injunction", to stop presentation or to stop advertisement, to last until after the hearing of the "with notice" application, for which the court will then fix a date.

The without notice application for an "interim injunction"

The company should then very speedily prepare an application for an "interim injunction", and the witness statement or statements in support (see below). In addition to putting the company's case for disputing the creditor's claim, and asking the court to stop the presentation or advertisement of the petition, their evidence should describe what efforts the company has made with the creditor's solicitors to obtain their agreement to hold it up. The Forms of application for an injunction are printed in the Appendix at pages 198 and 200 below.

When the papers are ready (in the form explained below), they should be taken to the court, with the fee and application to the court officials should be made for a without notice hearing before the judge, explaining the urgency.

If the company's without notice application for an interim injunction is granted

If the company's without notice application is granted, and the court makes an order for an interim injunction, the company should at once inform the creditor's solicitors by phone, and also by post or e-mail, of the terms of the order. The creditor will then be served with the papers for the hearing of the with notice application, the date for which the judge will have fixed, and which the order will specify, as the date when the interim injunction will finish.

To persuade the court to make either of these orders, the company has to show good reasons. The company's success in preventing the petition being presented depends on how good are the reasons put forward for objecting to the debt.

Once a petition has been presented and served on the company, the court is generally unwilling to prevent it being advertised. The reason for this is that, if the company turns out to be unable to pay its debts as they fall due (as the petition claims), it is thought that, in the public interest, the business public must be warned, by the advertisement, about dealing with the company.

For the Court Forms to use to apply for injunctions, and the procedure, see pages 198, 200 and 202 in the Appendix, below. The court officials will tell you the court fee.

The evidence to support the applications

The grounds of opposition to the statutory demand must be set out in one or more **witness statements, verified by statements of truth:** as to how to prepare these, see Chapter 10, above.

A specimen witness statement is included in the Appendix, at page 202, below; this is included to show how the statement must be laid out.

Procedure for filing and making a "with notice" application for an injunction

When the company's application for an injunction of either sort is ready with the evidence and exhibits completed, it should be filed in court, with the fee paid, and with an additional copy for the court, and copies prepared for the creditor or his solicitors, accompanied by the original witness statement, with its original exhibits.

A copy of the witness statement and of its exhibits should be sent or delivered to the creditor's solicitors, if they are identified in the statutory demand or the petition, **not less than 14 days before the date fixed for the hearing of the application.**

The creditor's evidence in reply

If the creditor wishes to reply to, or to challenge, the company's evidence, he must file his witness statements in court, and send copies to the company, **not less than seven days before the date fixed for the hearing.**

Cross-examination on witness statements: applying for permission

If the company, or the creditor, wishes to cross-examine any of one another's witnesses at the hearing, each of them must apply to the court for an order that the witnesses shall attend the hearing for that purpose: see further below.

Application to the court for permission to cross-examine witnesses is made on an "ordinary application" (Court Form 7.2): see Appendix, page 195, below. The court officials will tell you the court fee.

Who hears the application for the injunction?

Since the company's application is for an injunction, which only the judge can order, the application must be heard by the judge, and not by the Registrar or the District Judge.

The representation of the company in court on the hearing of its application

See Chapter 31, page 145 below, for the procedure to obtain the judge's consent for the company or the partnership to appear not by a lawyer but by a non-legal representative.

The hearing of the application: the hearing day

The company's representative must arrive in court in good time, with all the copies of documents, the company's own and the creditor's, which he will need to read or to consult, and the judge's consent for him to appear. He should hand this last item in to the court usher, identifying himself as the company's representative. He should also introduce himself to the lawyers appearing for the creditor.

Presence of witnesses for cross-examination

If permission to cross-examine witnesses has been given, he should find out whether the witnesses for the creditor, whom the company has required to be present for cross-examination, are, or will be, present, and when. He should also confirm that those of the company's witnesses whom the creditor has required to be present for cross-examination are present, or if not present, when they will arrive.

The hearing of the application

When the name of the case is called, the company has the right to begin, and its representative should then briefly explain its case to the judge. The judge will probably have read all the witness statements already, in which case the judge will say that he does not need them to be read in full; the representative need only refer to the most important parts that the company relies on.

The representative will offer for cross-examination the witnesses asked for by the creditor. When they have been cross-examined, he can then "re-examine" them, that is, ask questions seeking to correct any parts of the evidence which the cross-examination has damaged.

When the company's case has been completed, the creditor's lawyers will then put his case, and offer their witnesses for cross-examination.

If the creditor's lawyers are going to read from any lawbooks or any law reports in support of their case, they should have sent the company a list of these before the hearing, with photocopies of the passages which they are going to read.

At the close of the creditor's evidence and arguments, the company's representative is entitled to reply.

Possible settlement of the case

It is possible that during the hearing there will be discussions about a possible settlement. The company should therefore have in court someone who is authorised to discuss and to enter into a settlement. Unless the representative is himself a director, able to make decisions on behalf of the board, or a director is otherwise present, it would be convenient for the representative to have been specifically authorised in writing by the company to act for it in this matter. Any agreement made by him will then be binding on the company.

Judgment: if the company's application succeeds

If the judge gives judgment on the company's application wholly in the company's favour, he will make an order for a permanent injunction, barring the presentation of any winding-up petition for the debt in question, or striking out the petition if presented; he will usually also order the creditor to pay the company's costs of the application, which are sometimes "assessed" by the judge (that is, the amount of costs is decided) there and then.

If the judge decides only to stop the advertisement, he may award the company costs, if the creditor has argued that the advertisement should be allowed; otherwise, he will reserve the costs to the hearing of the petition.

Costs

For the costs allowable to the company, when appearing in person, see Chapter 31 at page 147, below.

If the injunction application is refused

If the company has applied to prevent a winding-up petition being presented, the creditor will now present it. He cannot add the amount of any costs that he has been awarded to the debt claimed in the petition, which must be for the same amount as was claimed in the demand.

If the company has only applied for an injunction to prevent advertisement of the petition, which has already been served, the creditor will be directed to advertise the petition, and a new date will be fixed for the hearing.

Opposing the petition

The company must now prepare to oppose the petition, on any grounds which are still open to it, after it has failed to prevent its presentation or its advertisement.

Any further witness statements, with their exhibits, verified by statements of truth, should be made and filed in court, with a spare copy for the court, **not less than seven days before the date fixed for the hearing.** Copies should be served on the creditor, or his solicitors.

If the company has made an injunction application to the court, then the witness statements which supported it should be referred to: they will be on the court file.

For the procedure at the hearing, see Chapter 32, page 149, below.

CHAPTER 31

HOW A COMPANY CAN APPEAR IN COURT "IN PERSON"

Until recently, a company could only be represented in court in a law case, in which it was a party, by a barrister or a solicitor.

Since a company cannot get legal aid, and cannot easily qualify for being represented in court by one of the legal charity organisations (see Chapter 25, above), a small company which is too short of funds to employ lawyers has difficulty in defending itself, or in enforcing its rights, unless financed by its directors or its shareholders, or unless it can obtain the services of solicitors in the form of a "contingency fees agreement" (a "CFA"), the so-called "no win, no fee agreement" : see also Chapter 25, above.

However, if the company cannot obtain legal representation in court to present its case or to defend itself, the law now permits a company to appear "in person" (as a human litigant can do), by a representative, though this needs the consent of the court. It can be represented in court by an "employee", a term which seems to be treated as including a director.

Application for the consent of the court must be applied for **before the hearing**; it may be applied for informally, without reference to other parties. The court officials will help with the procedure.

It is assumed that the provisions made for the benefit of limited companies, as above, apply equally to partnerships, which are to be wound-up as unregistered companies.

How to apply for the consent of the court

Application should be made, if possible, to the judge who will be hearing the case; in the case of a winding-up petition, this will be a

Registrar or a District Judge. If that particular judge is not available, application can be made to another judge of that rank.

The Court Rules recommend that consent should be given, unless there is some sufficient or particular reason for refusing it. The judge must take into account the complexity of the case, and the experience, and the position in the company, of the person proposed as the company's representative. If the judge gives his consent, he must record it in writing, and must provide the company (and any other party who asks for one) with a copy of his written consent.

How to apply for leave to appear

If the proceedings, in which the company is to appear, have already started with the service (that is, the issue) by the company, or on the company, of legal court documents, the application must be made on an "ordinary application" (Court Form 7.2) printed in the Appendix at page 195. If proceedings have not yet started, application must be made on an "Originating application" (Court Form 7.1) page 193. A fee is presumably chargeable on the application, which the court officials will tell you.

At the hearing, the company must provide the court with a written statement, giving the following information:

(1) the full name of the company, as stated in its certificate of incorporation;
(2) the company's registered name;
(3) the position of, or the office in the company held by, the representative who has been authorised to appear;
(4) the date when the representative was authorised to appear for the company, and by what means he was authorised, such as a written authority from the managing director, or a Board resolution, giving its date in each case.

Since human litigants in person are entitled to have in court to support them a "lay adviser" (that is, a person who is not a lawyer), it would seem that a company should be entitled to have one too; the application should therefore include his name and profession. Lay advisers can only advise the company's representative; only very rarely are they allowed to address the court.

Costs of the company appearing in person

A company which appears without a legal representative is a litigant in person, for the purposes of the rules regulating the costs claimable by litigants in person: see Chapter 3 at page 9.

CHAPTER 32
THE HEARING OF THE WINDING-UP PETITION

Note: *References in this chapter to a company apply to a partnership, unless otherwise stated.*

One of the important differences between the bankruptcy procedure and the winding-up procedure is that the bankruptcy procedure almost always excludes any advertisement of, or the giving of any publicity to, the presentation of the bankruptcy petition (except by way of a notice outside the court on the day of the hearing).

Because of the absence of advertisement of a bankruptcy petition, (except in very rare cases), the hearing is usually limited to a contest between the petitioning creditor and the debtor, and takes place in private, on a one-to-one basis. However, other creditors of the debtor, who have become aware of the hearing of the petition, can give notice of their desire to attend and to take part in the petition.

The winding-up procedure is different. Unless an order has been made preventing the advertisement of the petition, the advertisement will have invited other creditors of the company to attend the hearing and to take part in it, for or against the petitioning creditor's application for the company to be wound up.

Other creditors may still attend, even when the petition has not been advertised, if they have heard, from other sources, such as trade or professional journals, that a winding-up petition against the company is fixed for hearing. However, "outside creditors" do not often attend hearings of winding-up petitions.

Another important difference is that the petition is heard by the Registrar or the District Judge in public, i.e. in open court.

Representation of the company in court

If the company has been unable to pay for, or otherwise to obtain, legal representation for its defence against the petition, it can apply to the court for the consent of a judge for the company to appear in court by a duly authorised representative: see Chapter 31, above. It is assumed that the provisions apply equally to partnerships.

Attendance of other creditors

Where other creditors of the company have learned of the hearing of the petition, and wish to take part in the hearing, they must, before the hearing, give written notice to the petitioning creditor of their intention to appear at the hearing, stating their debt, and whether they intend to support the petition or to oppose it.

The list of creditors attending the hearing of the petition

The petitioning creditor must prepare a list of the names and addresses of any creditors who have given him notice of their intention to attend the hearing, stating whether they intend to support or oppose the petition, the amounts of their debts, and the names of their solicitors (if any), and they must supply copies of the list to the court and to the company.

Creditors who have given notice of their intention to attend the hearing are entitled to put in evidence by witness statement, stating their views as to whether the company should or should not be wound up, or what other order should be made on the petition.

They must file their witness statements with the court, and supply copies to the petitioning creditor and to the company.

Possible substitution of petitioning creditor

If the petitioning creditor has failed to advertise the petition, or does not appear at the hearing, or has made a settlement or an agreement with the company, which would lead to the petition being dismissed, withdrawn, or allowed to be adjourned, another creditor who is present and has given notice of his intention to take part in the hearing, and who is owed a sufficient debt currently due from the company, and is otherwise qualified, can apply to the court to be "substituted" as petitioning creditor. A shareholder can also apply to be substituted.

The court can also, in such a case, make a "change of carriage order" in favour of another creditor, or a shareholder, who is then allowed to carry on with the existing petition.

When a substitution of a new petitioning creditor, or a shareholder, is ordered by the court, the petition proceedings will go on, with the substituted creditor or shareholder as the new petitioning creditor or petitioner. The petition before the court will be amended to show the new petitioning creditor or shareholder, the new debt and other necessary particulars.

The proceedings will be adjourned, to give the company time to deal with the claim of the new petitioning creditor, and to present its defence to that claim.

The hearing of the petition: the hearing day

The company's representative should arrive at court punctually, with all the papers necessary to conduct the company's defence to the petition, including the creditor's witness statements and exhibits, and any photocopies of law books or law reports which the creditor's solicitors have supplied the company with.

He should also have with him details of the debts owed by the company to the other creditors who have given notice to attend, so that he will be able to deal with any case they put up against the company, or if they should wish to settle with the company.

If the company has already made an application to the court through its representative, such as for an injunction, he will have then handed into court his copy of a judge's consent to the company being represented by himself, which the judge will be likely to have kept. He should ask the court usher to check this. If the consent has not been handed in before, then it should be handed in to the court usher now.

Other creditors attending the hearing of the petition

If the company has received from the creditor's solicitors a list of other creditors of the company who have given notice of their intention to attend, he should identify them, if present, should introduce himself as the company's representative, and should ask whether they are legally represented, and what part they intend to take in the hearing of the petition. There may be one creditor, or more than one, who will be opposed to the company being wound-up, and could become the representative's allies at the hearing, in opposing the petition.

At the hearing of the petition, in public, the creditor, or his lawyers, will begin, presenting his case and reading the witness statements they have filed in support of the petition, and in opposition to any application which the company has made for an injunction.

The company's representative may need to cross-examine on the creditor's witness statements, if permission has been given to cross-examine. He should have prepared a list of the questions he feels it necessary to ask, with all relevant references to the documents in evidence.

Creditors who have given notice to attend the hearing, and who wish to be heard, for or against the petition, will then be heard, and their evidence (if any) will be read, and possibly cross-examined to.

The company's case will then be opened by its representative, and its evidence will be read, so far as the judge requires it to be read, and will be cross-examined to, if permission has been given.

If the creditor proposes to read any law books or to refer to any law reports, in support of his case, his solicitors should have given a list of them to the court, and to the company, before the hearing. If the company is appearing in person (see above), the solicitors should have supplied the company, before the hearing, with photocopies of passages they propose to read.

Re-examination

After a witness has been cross-examined on his witness statement, the creditor, or his lawyers, or the company's representative, are entitled to ask their witness questions in re-examination, to try to clear up disputed matters raised in cross-examination.

At the end of the company's evidence and arguments, the creditor is entitled to reply and to sum up.

How the balance of creditors' debts affects the judgment

The court does not, at the end of the hearing, mathematically balance the amounts of the debts of creditors supporting and those opposing the petition, although the totals on each side are an important general factor for concluding the judgment on the petition. The court may well decide in favour of the side with a somewhat lower amount of debts in support.

The judgment on the petition

The court will usually deliver judgment at the end of the arguments, but it may adjourn the hearing for the delivery of judgement on a later day.

If the court is minded to make a winding-up order, and the company has the funds available, immediately or almost immediately, to pay off the debt, its representative can ask for a brief adjournment to give it the time to pay.

However, such a payment to avert the making of a winding-up order and to dismiss the petition, will generally not be approved and accepted by the court, nor be agreed to, unless the funds being used are proved to be third-party money.

The making of the winding-up order

If the court makes a winding-up order, it will order that the costs of the petitioning creditor are to be paid out of the assets in the winding-up. The order will appoint the Official Receiver to be the first liquidator: see Chapter 33, page 155, below.

If the company succeeds in defeating the petition

If the court finds in the company's favour, it will dismiss the petition, with an order that the company's costs are to be payable by the creditor. Those costs can be set off against any debt that has been established to be due by the company.

Appeal

The company is entitled to appeal against the making of a winding-up order, but only with the permission of the court. The creditor whose petition is dismissed, or where the hearing of it is adjourned, contrary to his wishes and interest, is also entitled to appeal. The notice of appeal must be filed within 21 days.

If the company wishes to appeal against the winding-up order, its representative can ask the court to "stay", that is, postpone the operation of the order, pending the hearing of the appeal; but the court will require good reasons for agreeing to this, and an indication of which parts of its judgment the company disagrees with, and will impose strict conditions on the company as to its actions during the postponement.

For the procedure after the making of a winding-up order, see Chapter 33, page 155, below.

CHAPTER 33

HOW THE WINDING-UP ORDER AFFECTS YOU AND YOUR FELLOW DIRECTORS, OFFICERS OR PARTNERS

When the court makes a winding-up order against the company or the partnership, its effect is to automatically appoint the Official Receiver to be its "liquidator". He will hold this position and exercise all the powers attached to it, until the creditors have been summoned by him to a meeting, at which they are entitled to vote, and have voted to appoint an "outside liquidator"; if there is no creditors' meeting held to appoint a liquidator, or a liquidator is not appointed at the meeting which was held, the Official Receiver will remain the liquidator.

The Official Receiver will send the company or the partnership a copy of the winding-up order sealed by the court as soon as he receives copies of it from the court; but the order takes effect from the moment when it is made, the precise time being noted by the court.

The Statement of Affairs

The Official Receiver almost invariably requires the persons who have been running the company, or the partnership, to prepare, and verify under oath, a "statement of affairs".

He sends an official notice to those people whom he considers to be in a position to make the statement, or to concur in making it, and specifies the time within which it must be submitted to him.

This is an important date which must be met, or an offence will have been committed; but the time can be extended by the Official

Receiver, or he may release the obligation to make or to concur in making the statement.

If the Official Receiver refuses, when the company applies to him, to extend the time, or to release the obligation on any of the other persons required to make, or to concur in making, the statement, application can be made to the court for an order. For an ordinary application form for this purpose, see Appendix, at page 195, below. The court officials will tell you the fee.

Persons liable to be required to make the statement of affairs

The persons who can be required to make, or to concur in making, the statement of affairs are the following:

(a) Present or former directors or officers of the company, or partners in or officers of the partnership;
(b) Persons who took part in the formation of the company or the partnership at any time within one year before the date of the winding-up order, or of the appointment of a provisional liquidator;
(c) Present or past employees, whom the Official Receiver thinks capable of giving the required information;
(d) Persons who are, or have during that year been, officers or employees of a company which is, or within that year was, an officer of the company.

The Official Receiver's notice must give the names and addresses of all the other persons who have been required to make or to concur in making the statement. The notice must also inform the person notified of their duty to provide him with information, and to attend on him, if required. Failure to provide information, or to attend on him, is an offence.

Contents of the statement of affairs

The statement is required to deal with the following matters:

(a) particulars of the company's assets, debts and liabilities;
(b) the names and addresses of the company's creditors;
(c) any securities held by the creditors over the property of the company, and the dates when those securities were given;

(d) any further information which may be ordered to be given or which the Official Receiver may require.

The Official Receiver will supply the forms for preparing the statement, with instructions on how they are to be completed.

The costs of making the statement of affairs

If a person required to prepare the statement, or to concur in it, cannot prepare it himself, the Official Receiver may, at the expense of the assets, employ someone else to prepare it, or to prepare an affidavit to state that person's concurrence. He may alternatively authorise the payment of an allowance out of the assets towards expenses to be incurred by that person in employing some other named person or firm to prepare it, or the concurrence in it.

"Qualified concurrence"

A person required to concur in a statement of affairs prepared by others may "qualify his affidavit of concurrence", that is, he may express his disagreement with what the statement says, or he may withhold his agreement, where he is not in agreement with the statement as made, or thinks it to be erroneous or misleading, or where he is without the direct knowledge necessary for him to be able to concur.

Delivery of the statement of affairs

When the statement is ready, it must be verified by affidavit, and delivered to the Official Receiver, with a copy. Affidavits of concurrence must be delivered by the makers to the Official Receiver, with a copy of each. The affidavits may be sworn before any Official Receiver or Deputy Official Receiver, or a court official authorised to take oaths, without fee.

Submission of accounts

Any of the persons who are liable to be required to make a statement of affairs may be required by the liquidator to prepare and submit accounts of the company, in such form and for whatever period as he may specify.

As is the case with the Official Receiver assisting with the expenses of preparing the statement of affairs (see above), the liquidator may, at the cost of the assets, employ someone to provide help with the accounts, or make an allowance towards the cost of employing someone to help with them.

Duty to give further assistance

The Official Receiver may at any time require the persons liable to make the statement of affairs to provide him with further information amplifying, modifying or explaining any matter contained in the statement of affairs, or in any of the accounts.

The Official Receiver may require the required information to be supplied in writing, and to be verified by affidavit. When ready, it must be supplied in two copies, and delivered to the Official Receiver within 21 days of his request, or such longer period as he may allow.

Meetings of creditors and contributories

If the Official Receiver decides to call meetings of the creditors and the shareholders, for the purposes of their voting to appoint a liquidator, and for other formal winding-up business, he, or whoever else is convening the meetings, must give notice to such of the people described above as being liable to make the statement of affairs as he thinks should be told of the meetings or should be present at either of them. He may give notice to some of them that they are required to attend, which they must punctually do.

Delivery up of company property

If you or your colleagues are in possession of any of the company's property, it must be promptly delivered up to the Official Receiver or the liquidator, depending on who asks for it.

CHAPTER 34

THE COURT CAN EXAMINE PEOPLE CONCERNED WITH THE COMPANY OR PARTNERSHIP ABOUT ITS AFFAIRS

In Chapter 15, page 57, above, the powers were explained which the court has to examine bankrupts, their wives, civil partners or partners, and other people about the affairs of the bankrupt. These powers include the ordering of both a public examination of the bankrupt and private examinations.

The court has the same powers of examination in the case of the winding-up of a company or an insolvent partnership.

You, your fellow directors (or fellow partners in the case of a partnership) and any other officers (such as the secretary or a manager), and any other people who were involved in promoting or setting up the company or the partnership, can be ordered by the court to attend at the court to be publicly examined, on oath, about the affairs of the company or the partnership, its assets, its debts, and how it became insolvent and came to be wound-up.

At a public examination, the person being examined can be questioned by the Official Receiver, the liquidator, any creditor who has put in a proof of debt, and any shareholder. The persons being examined can be represented by a lawyer, if available.

The court can also order a private examination on oath of you or of any of those people, and of any other person whom the court thinks to be capable of giving information about the formation, business affairs or dealings of the company or the partnership.

Such examinations can also include the wives, husbands, civil partners or partners of those people. Private examinations are held in private.

Any person who is summoned to be privately examined by the court may be ordered to make an affidavit of his dealings with the company or the partnership, and to produce any books, papers or records which he holds, relating to those dealings.

Answers made to questions put to people being publicly examined may be used against them in later proceedings, and so may the answers made to questions put at private examinations.

If, when examined at an examination, you consider any question to be unfair, you may complain to the judge, and ask that you be excused from answering it. At the end of the examination, you can make a statement, on your own behalf, about any matters which the persons questioning you have not sufficiently cleared up, or of which they gave an incorrect or unfair explanation or description.

Failure, without a good excuse, to attend a public examination or a private examination is an offence, for which the person may be prosecuted.

CHAPTER 35
DISQUALIFICATION OF COMPANY DIRECTORS AND PARTNERS

Where a company has become insolvent, whether being in winding-up or in administration, and a director of the company is found by the court, on an application made by the Secretary of State for Trade and Industry, or by the Official Receiver acting on his or her behalf, to have behaved in a manner that makes him unfit to be concerned in the management of a company, he may be disqualified by order of the court for a period between two and fifteen years.

Under a "disqualification order", he is disqualified from being a director of a company, or acting as the receiver of a company's assets, or in any way, directly or indirectly, being concerned in or taking part in the promotion, formation or management of a company, without the leave of a court.

Instead of obtaining a disqualification order from the court, the Secretary of State may accept from the director a "disqualification undertaking". Under this, the director undertakes not, without the leave of a court, to do any of the things which he would be prohibited from doing under a disqualification order.

Breaches of a disqualification order or undertaking expose the person bound by them to prosecution and punishment by imprisonment or a fine. In addition, if he has been managing a company while disqualified, he is liable for the company's debts, incurred while he was managing it.

Similar orders and undertakings have now been introduced into bankruptcy: see Chapter 22, page 95, above.

Partnerships

Similar orders to those capable of being made against a director of an insolvent company, can be made against, and similar undertakings can be accepted, from an officer in an insolvent partnership whose conduct of the partnership business is held by the court to have made him unfit to be concerned in the management of a company. For this purpose, a member of a partnership is deemed to be the director of an unregistered company, under which description the partnership may be wound up.

There are now "Limited Liability Partnerships", whose management and control fall midway between a company and an unlimited partnership, and whose members are subject to similar orders and undertakings.

CHAPTER 36

CRIMINAL OFFENCES WITH WHICH DIRECTORS, OFFICERS OR PARTNERS CAN BE CHARGED

After a company or an insolvent partnership has been ordered to be wound-up by the court, officers (including directors) and partners become liable to be prosecuted for criminal offences committed by them before the winding up, or in the course of the proceedings, or in the course of the winding-up.

These offences substantially resemble those capable of being committed by debtors before the making of the bankruptcy order, or during the bankruptcy: see Chapter 16, page 59, above. The offences relate to such instances of criminal misconduct as the concealment or wrongful removal of the company's property, concealment of or damage to the company's accounts, the pawning of the company's property, committing frauds on the creditors and the failure to make due disclosure to the liquidator.

There are "statutory defences" to charges for such offences, that the person charged had no intent to defraud, or to conceal the state of affairs of the company or the partnership, or to defeat the law.

CHAPTER 37

RELATIONS BETWEEN THE LIQUIDATOR AND THE OFFICERS OF THE COMPANY OR THE PARTNERSHIP

The making of the winding-up order against the company or the partnership automatically appoints the Official Receiver to be its liquidator. He or she will hold that office until a meeting of the creditors is held (if it is decided to summon one) to appoint an "outside liquidator".

Unlike the position of a trustee in bankruptcy, who, on his appointment, becomes the owner in law of all of the bankrupt's property, (see Chapter 17, above), the liquidator does not become the absolute owner of the company's or the partnership's property, but does become its absolute manager and trustee of it.

The Official Receiver is a highly qualified public official of the Insolvency Service; the outside liquidator will be a licensed insolvency practitioner, also highly qualified, and subject to the control of the court if he misconducts himself, or acts unjustly or unfairly.

Importance of relations with the liquidator

The directors and officers of the company or the partnership which is being wound-up will be well-advised to set up, and to maintain, very good relations with the liquidator, whether he is the Official Receiver or an outside liquidator.

The goodwill of the liquidator is important, in hopefully inclining him to the view that the directors and officers of the company or the partnership have done their best for the survival of the company, and for the preserving of the interests of the creditors, even if in the end they did not succeed.

Prompt and full compliance with all the liquidator's requests for information, documents, or the location and identification of the company's property or stock, will be welcome. This course of conduct may help to reduce the possibility of the Official Receiver applying for a public examination of any of the directors and officers, and of the liquidator applying for private examinations of them, or their wives, husbands, civil partners or partners.

The liquidator's goodwill could also be important, if there is a possibility that the company may be accused of having entered into transactions at an undervalue, which should be set aside: see Chapter 38, page 167, below. To such charges, there is a defence; the court may not make an order in such a case, if it is satisfied that the company acted in good faith, and for the benefit of the company; to establish those facts, a well-disposed liquidator could be a helpful witness.

The most important field in which the attitude of the liquidator could be crucial is when he has to decide whether the directors or officers have acted so unsatisfactorily as to require him to report them to the Department of Trade and Industry, with a view to disqualification proceedings being taken.

CHAPTER 38

PAST TRANSACTIONS BY THE COMPANY OR THE PARTNERSHIP, WHICH MAY BE SET ASIDE AGAINST DIRECTORS AND OTHERS

The liquidator of a company or a partnership in insolvent winding-up has the duty to investigate the company's activities, to check whether any of its transactions were carried out within various periods before the winding-up, at a time when the company or partnership was insolvent, or is to be treated as having been insolvent, which were carried out either:

(1) at an undervalue, that is, either for nothing, as a gift, or at a substantially less valuable return in exchange for what was handed over; or
(2) by way of preference of one (or more than one) creditor, over the rest of the creditors.

If he finds that there have been such transactions, he must apply to the court to set them aside. Before doing so, he may apply to the court to privately examine the persons who did the transactions on each side: see Chapter 34, page 159, above.

The law in winding-up as to setting aside such transactions done at an under-value, or done by way of preferring a creditor, is substantially the same as the law in bankruptcy, which is discussed at Chapter 21, page 87, above.

There is, however, an important difference between the two laws. In the case of a transaction done at an undervalue by a company later wound-up as insolvent, the court must not set the transaction aside, if it is satisfied that (1) the company entered into the transaction in good faith, and for the purpose of carrying on its business, and

(2) that when it did the transaction, there were reasonable grounds for believing that the transaction would benefit the company.

Transactions done by the company with an "associate" (a person or a company, though not an employee: see Chapter 21, page 87, above), are more strictly dealt with by the court from the point of view of setting them aside, and the periods of time relative to that process are longer than those applicable to transactions done with a stranger, who is in no way associated with the company.

CHAPTER 39

CLAIMS AGAINST DIRECTORS AND OTHERS FOR DAMAGES OR CONTRIBUTIONS TO THE ASSETS

As already mentioned in Chapter 26, page 123 above, directors, officers and other people concerned with the formation and running of a company or a partnership may be held liable to contribute to its assets, after it has gone into insolvent winding-up, if they have behaved badly, fraudulently or negligently in conducting its affairs, business, or trading.

The types of misbehaviour which may make them liable are labelled as **Misfeasance, Fraudulent Trading and Wrongful Trading.**

Misfeasance

This term applies to a person who is or has been an officer of the company (or has acted as its liquidator or administrative receiver), or is or has been concerned with, or has taken part in, its promotion, formation or management. If such a person has misapplied or retained or become accountable for any money or other property of the company, or has been guilty of any misfeasance (that is, serious misconduct) or breach of any fiduciary duty (that is, a breach of trust) or other duty in relation to the company, he may be examined by the court, and may be ordered to repay or restore or account for the money or property or any part of it by way of compensation.

Fraudulent Trading

If, in the course of the winding-up of a company, it appears that any business of the company has been carried on with intent to defraud the creditors of the company, or the creditors of anyone else, or for any fraudulent purpose, the court may hold any persons who were knowingly parties to the carrying on of business in that manner liable to make contributions to the assets.

Wrongful Trading

Where a company has gone into insolvent winding-up, and, some time before the commencement of the winding-up, a person who is or has been a director, or a "shadow director", (see below), of the company knew or ought to have realised that there was no reasonable prospect that the company could avoid going into insolvent winding-up, the court may declare that person liable to contribute to the company's assets. The court will regard the facts which should have been known, and the steps which should have been taken, to be those which a reasonably diligent person would have known and taken.

But the court will not make such a declaration, if it is satisfied that when that person knew that the company was almost bound to go into insolvent winding-up, he took every step which he ought to have taken to reduce the loss which could accrue to the company's creditors.

A "shadow director" of a company is a person in accordance with whose directions or instructions the directors of the company are accustomed to act; the term does not include a person giving advice in a professional capacity.

CHAPTER 40

DISSOLUTION OF COMPANY: RESCISSION OF WINDING-UP ORDER

Unless the company can successfully appeal against the making of the winding-up order, or unless it enters into a creditors' voluntary arrangement, or enters into administration (see Chapters 41 and 42, pages 175, 177 below), the normal way in which a winding-up comes to an end is by the completion of the realisation of the assets, and the distribution of the proceeds among the creditors, with any surplus going to the shareholders.

When these processes have been completed, the liquidator will take steps for the company to be dissolved. When this takes place, the company wholly ceases to exist as a legal person. If, after it is dissolved, further assets of the company are discovered, they will legally belong to the Crown (that is, the Treasury), as property no longer belonging to anyone.

The shareholders can ask the Treasury to give up its claim to the assets, and if it does, they can apply to the court for an order that the property should be transferred to them.

The only other way in which a winding-up can be brought to an end is by obtaining from the court an order rescinding the winding-up order. This requires very strong grounds; but if there was a proposal to pay off all the debts of the company in full, this might be sufficient.

Such an application may also be made by a person who is an unsatisfied creditor of the company (or partnership), who was unaware of the winding-up proceedings.

PART VII
ALTERNATIVES TO
WINDING-UP

CHAPTER 41

THE COMPANY VOLUNTARY ARRANGEMENT : "THE CVA"

At Chapter 24 page 107, above there is a description of the procedure called "individual voluntary arrangement", which is a way for an insolvent person to try to settle with his creditors.

There is a similar procedure for insolvent companies, called a "company voluntary arrangement", often called "the CVA". The company appoints an insolvency practitioner, or a similarly qualified accountant, to prepare proposals to put before the company's creditors at a meeting. The proposals set out the company's plan to try to rescue itself, and what sums the creditors can expect to receive, less than the amount of their full debts.

The practitioner or accountant, called "the nominee", must express his personal belief in the proposals being likely to succeed in rescuing the company.

If the creditors approve the proposals by the necessary majority, this brings into existence an agreement between the company and each creditor who had notice of the proposed arrangement, whether or not they attended the meeting, and also an agreement between all the creditors, to accept the proposals.

The nominee then becomes "the supervisor", who administers the arrangement, and distributes the agreed dividends.

If the arrangement does not succeed, the supervisor may be obliged to petition for the winding-up of the company; he must also do so, if he finds that the company's officers have misled him and/or the creditors, as to the position of the company, its assets and its prospects.

CHAPTER 42
ADMINISTRATION

"Administration" is another procedure for providing a means to rescue a company or a partnership, which cannot pay its debts, but could be reconstructed and returned to solvency, or saved from a winding-up, by a different administration. It does not apply to individual bankrupts.

The procedure is complicated and expensive, and is only described here for completeness.

An administrator of a company or a partnership in difficulties can be appointed by the court on an application made by the company or the partnership, or by a creditor, or by a debenture holder: an administrator can also be appointed directly by a debenture holder, or by the company or its directors, or by the members of the partnership.

The administrator, if appointed, becomes the complete controller of the affairs of the company or the partnership, and prepares proposals to be made to the creditors for rescuing the company. During this procedure, the company or the partnership is protected from any proceedings against itself or its property by any of its creditors.

The administrator is entitled to exercise many of the powers of the liquidator, as described in Part VI.

CHAPTER 43

THE GOVERNMENT'S NEW PROCEDURES

The Government is at present very concerned at the very large amount of indebtedness currently owed by very large numbers of people, and steadily increasing, particularly among those classed as "consumer debtors", i.e. those whose indebtedness has been wholly, or very largely, incurred otherwise that in the course of a business.

With a view to reducing, so far as possible, the number of people liable to go bankrupt, or to have to go into individual voluntary arrangements (see Chapter 24, page 107 above), the government is proposing to set up additional procedures to assist them in dealing with their financial difficulties. It has introduced into Parliament a Bill to create a number of new means of helping debtors unable to pay their debts. The Bill is called the Tribunals, Courts and Enforcement Bill, 2006.

All but one of these new procedures will be restricted to debtors whose debts are "non-business debts". The Bill is expected to become law in the course of 2007, but the new procedures may not be put into operation until considerably later; many sets of regulations will need to be prepared and passed through Parliament. But the processes could be speeded up, if necessary.

The proposed new procedures are briefly summarized below.

NEW PROCEDURES FOR NON-BUSINESS DEBTORS

(1) A new form of administration order

This will replace the present administration order procedure in the county court, to be applied for by a debtor with at least two non-business debts, not exceeding a fixed amount, which he is unable to pay, and who has an income of not more than a fixed amount. The court will be able to make an order for him to pay his debts by instalments; the order will not be able to last for more than five years.

(2) Enforcement Restriction Orders

These orders will be restricted to debtors who have suffered a sudden and unforeseen worsening of their financial position, which can realistically be expected to improve within the six months following the date of the order. The Order will be applied for in the county court.

(3) Debt Management Schemes, operating Debt Management Plans.

Such Schemes will have to be approved by a "supervising authority", who will be either the Lord Chancellor, or some person or body authorized by him.

NEW PROCEDURES FOR DEBTORS, INCLUDING BUSINESS DEBTORS

(4) Debt Relief Orders

A debtor will be able to apply for an order that, effectively, he should be released from all his debts, except those secured by a mortgage, charge or lien.

The application will not be made to the court, but to the Official Receiver. It will have to be made by an "approved intermediary" on the debtor's behalf. That person will be an individual approved by a competent authority (designated by the Secretary of State for Trade and Industry) to act as an intermediary between the debtor and the Official Receiver.

The total amount of the debtor's indebtedness, his monthly surplus income (if any), and the value of his property, will in each case need not to exceed fixed amounts.

This is the scheme already nicknamed "NINA", (No income, no assets).

(5) Individual Voluntary Arrangements (see Chapter 24, above).

Consultations are going on to make these easier and cheaper; these changes might be brought in sooner than the new procedures above.

The intended effects of the Orders

The procedures to be laid down for applying for and obtaining the orders outlined above will in each case provide that when the order is made, the debtor will be protected from any other form of judgment enforcement, bankruptcy or insolvency process. The debtor will be subject to severe restrictions on his activities and dealings, and orders may be refused if he has behaved badly to his creditors.

APPENDIX

PART 1

Application to set aside statutory demand (IR 1986, r 6.4, Form 6.4)

IN THE HIGH COURT OF JUSTICE

or IN THE .... COUNTY COURT   No ..... of ..... 20 .....

IN BANKRUPTCY

Re [*full name or name and initials of debtor*] A Debtor

Ex parte the Debtor

To

Address

This application is served on you by the Debtor:

Name

Address

LET [*name of creditor issuing demand, and address*]
ATTEND BEFORE Mr Registrar ...... / the District Judge as
follows:

Date

Time
Place

on the hearing of an application by [*name of debtor*]   the
Applicant for an order that the Statutory Demand dated [*date*] to
be set aside.

The grounds on which the Applicant claims to be entitled to the
order are set out in the witness statement of the Applicant, a copy
of which statement accompanies this application.

The names and addresses of the persons upon whom this application should be served are: [*names and addresses of persons to be served*].

The Applicant's address for service is: [*address*]

DATED ....

SIGNED [*Applicant*] ....

If you do not attend, the Court may make such order as it thinks fit.

(Crown copyright)

Specimen Witness Statement in support of application to set aside statutory demand (IR 1986, r.6.4, Form 6.5)

[*Corner marking*]

IN THE HIGH COURT OF JUSTICE

or IN THE .... COUNTY COURT   No...... of ...... 20......

IN BANKRUPTCY

Re [*full name or name and initials of debtor*] A Debtor

Ex parte the Debtor   Arthur Brown

To: CD Company Limited

Address of (*registered office, or other address stated in demand*)

　　　This witness statement is served on you by the Debtor

Name: Arthur Brown

Address of (*registered office, or other address stated in demand*)

　　　I [Arthur Brown of .... , company director, being the Debtor served with the demand] say as follows:

1　　　That on [*date*] the Statutory demand exhibited hereto and marked 'AB 1' came into my hands.

2　　　That [*insert one of the 8 following alternatives, or if none of them are applicable, state grounds on which you claim that the statutory demand should be set aside*].

  (i)　I do not admit the debt because the goods for the price of which the demand was issued have never been delivered to me or to my business.

  (ii)　I admit the debt, but not that it is payable immediately, since the terms of the invoice were for payment three months after delivery, which will not expire until [*date*]. I exhibit, marked 'AB2', a copy of the said invoice dated [*date*].

  (iii)　I admit the debt as to £[*amount*], and that this is payable, but that the remainder is not immediately payable. I am prepared to pay the amount of £...... immediately to [*state person*].

(iv) I admit the debt and am prepared to secure or compound for it to the creditor's satisfaction by [*state nature of satisfaction*]: [e.g. entering into a second charge on my house at [*address*]].

OR

(v) I say that the debt is a secured debt [*give full details of security and its value*].

(vi) I have a counter-claim (or set-off or cross demand) for £ [*amount*] being a sum equal to (or exceeding) the claim in respect of [*here state grounds of counterclaim, etc.*] [e.g. being the estimated cost of repairs to my motorcar registration number caused by the petitioner's Ford van colliding with it, while delivering the goods].

(vii) I say that execution on the judgment of the Court has been stayed upon my having obtained from the Court permission to appeal by order dated [*date*].

(viii) I say that the demand does not comply with the Insolvency Rules in that .... [*state reason*].

I believe that the facts stated herein are true.

Dated the .... day of ....20.......

(Signed) ....

Notice by debtor of intention to oppose bankruptcy petition (IR 1986, r 6.21, Form 6.19)

IN THE HIGH COURT OF JUSTICE

or IN THE .... COUNTY COURT   No...... of ...... 20......

IN BANKRUPTCY

Re [*full name or name and initials of debtor*] A Debtor

Ex parte the Debtor

TAKE NOTICE that I [*name and address of debtor*] or [*the above-named Debtor*] intend(s) to oppose the application to make a bankruptcy order against me (or him) on the following grounds:

[*Grounds*]

The facts stated herein are true.

DATED ....

To the [*above-named*] Court and to the [*Solicitors for*] the Petitioner.

(Crown copyright)

Form of Debtor's bankruptcy petition (Form 6.27)

TITLE OF DEBTOR

(a)   Insert full name, address and occupation (if any) of debtor

1.
(a) _____

_____

_____

(b)   Insert in full any other names by which the debtor is or has been known

also known as
(b) _____

(c)   Insert former address or addresses at which the debtor may have incurred debts or liabilities still unpaid or unsatisfied

[lately residing at
(c) _____

_____

(d)   Insert trading name (adding "with another or others", if this is so), business address and nature of the business

[and carrying on business as (d) _____

_____

_____

(e)   Insert any former trading names (adding "with another or others", if this is so), business address and nature of the business in respect of which the debtor may have incurred debts or liabilities still unpaid or unsatisfied

[and lately carrying on business as (e) _____

_____

_____

_____]

request the court that a bankruptcy order be made against me and say as follows:

(f)   Delete as applicable

1. (f) [My centre of main interests has been] [I have had an establishment] at

_____

OR

I carry on business as an insurance undertaking; a credit institution; investment undertaking providing services involving the holding of funds or securities for third parties; or a collective investment undertaking as referred to in Article 1.2 of the EC Regulation.

OR

My centre of main interests is not within a Member State

Under the EU Regulation:

(i) Centre of main interests should correspond to the place where the debtor conducts the administration of his interests on a regular basis.

(ii) Establishment is defined in the Council Regulation (No. 1346/2000) on insolvency proceedings as "any place of operations where the debtor carries out a non-transitory economic activity with human means and goods".

2. I have for the greater part of six months immediately preceding the presentation of this petition (f) [resided at] [carried on business at]

_____

_____

(g)   Insert name of court   within the district of (f) [this court] (g)   county court. I am presenting my petition to this court, as it is the nearest full-time county court to (g)   county court, for the following reasons:

(h)   State reasons   (h)

3. I am unable to pay my debts

4. (f) That within the period of five years ending with the date of this petition:

(j)   Insert date   _____

(i) I have not been adjudged bankrupt.

(k)   Insert name of court   OR

I was adjudged bankrupt on (j)   in the (k)

(l)   Insert number of bankruptcy proceedings   Court No. (1)

(ii) I have not (f) [made a composition with my creditors in satisfaction of my debts] or (f) [entered into a scheme of arrangement with creditors] (S 16 BA 1914)

OR
On (j)   I (f) [made a composition] [entered into a scheme of arrangement] with my creditors

(iii) I have not entered into a voluntary arrangement

OR
On (j)   I entered into a voluntary arrangement

(iv) I have not been subject to an administration order under Part VI of the County courts Act 1984

OR
On (j)   an administration order was made against me in
(l)   the county court

5. A statement of my affairs is filed with this petition.

Date _____

Signature _____

Complete only if petition
not heard immediately

Endorsement

This petition having been presented to the court on

_____

It is ordered that the petition shall be heard as follows:

Date _____

Time _____ hours

Place _____

Originating application (IR 1986, r 7.2, Form 7.1)

IN THE HIGH COURT OF JUSTICE

IN THE .... COUNTY COURT   No......... of 20.......

Re [*full name or name and initials of debtor*] A Debtor

Or

In the matter of .... Limited and in the matter of the Insolvency Act 1986

Between   Applicant

                                and

                                Respondent

LET [*name and address of respondent*] attend before the Judge / Mr Registrar .... /the District Judge at the above-named court on:

Date   at

Time   hours

Place [*address of court*]

On the hearing of an application by [*name and address of applicant*] the Applicant for an order in the following terms:

[*State the terms of the order to which the applicant claims to be entitled*]

The grounds on which the Applicant claims to be entitled to the order are:

[*Set out grounds or refer to a witness statement in support*]

The names and address of the persons upon whom it is intended to serve this application are:

[*State the names and addresses of the persons intended to be served*]

[*Or*]

It is not intended to serve any person with this application. The applicant's address for service is: [*address*]

DATED   SIGNED

                                       Applicant

Note: This Form is for applications to the court before the petition
is presented

Ordinary application (IR 1986, r 7.2, Sch 4,Form 7.2)

IN THE HIGH COURT OF JUSTICE

IN THE .... COUNTY COURT   No......... of 20.......

IN BANKRUPTCY

Re [*full name or name and initials of debtor*] A Debtor [*A Bankrupt*]

Or

In the matter of .... Limited and in the matter of the Insolvency Act 1986

Between   Applicant

                                 and

                                 Respondent

TAKE NOTICE that I / We [*name and address of applicant*] intend to apply to the Judge / Mr Registrar / the District Judge on:

Date

Time   hours

Place

For [*state nature and grounds of application or refer to a witness statement in support*]

SIGNED

            Applicant

My / Our address for service is:

To: [*give the name)(s) and address(es) of the person(s) (including the respondent) on whom it is intended to serve the application*]

[*Or*]

It is not intended to serve any person with this application

If you do not attend, the court will make such order as it thinks fit.

Note: _This Form is for applications to the court after the petition is presented._

Notice under Section 279 (2) of the Insolvency Act 1986 (IR 1986, r 6.214A, Sch 4, the Official Receiver's Notice)

Notice under Section 279 (2) of the Insolvency Act 1986

(TITLE)

A bankruptcy order having been made by this court against

(a)   Insert full   (a) _____
name and address
of bankrupt   _____

_____

_____

(b)   Insert date   on (b) _____
of bankruptcy order

Pursuant to section 279(2) of the Insolvency Act 1986, the Official Receiver states that the investigation of the bankrupt's affairs is unnecessary or concluded.

Dated ....

[Deputy] Official Receiver

of ....

DATE OF FILING AT COURT ....
(To be completed by court)

Notice to bankrupt

With effect from the date that this notice is filed in court, you are discharged from bankruptcy.

If you require a formal Certificate of Discharge, please contact the court.

Even though you are discharged from bankruptcy, you have a continuing duty pursuant to section 333 of the Insolvency Act 1986 to co-operate with the trustee in bankruptcy so that the trustee may carry out his functions. You also have a continuing duty pursuant to section 291 of the Insolvency Act 1986 to co-operate with the Official Receiver regarding the administration of your bankruptcy estate. You should further note that the assets in your bankruptcy estate remain vested in your trustee in bankruptcy and they will not be returned to you.

If you fail to co-operate with the trustee without a reasonable excuse, you are liable to be held in contempt of court and punished accordingly, and you may be sent to prison.

ORIGINATING APPLICATION to restrain presentation of winding-up petition

Either, *in the High Court:*

IN THE HIGH COURT OF JUSTICE   No........ of ....20 ......

Chancery Division
[Companies Court]
[........... District Registry]

Or, *in the county court:*

IN THE .... COUNTY COURT   No........ of ....20 ......

Then, *in any case:*

In the Matter of A.B. Ltd
And in the Matter of the Insolvency Act 1986

Between A.B. Ltd   Applicant

and

C.D. Ltd   Respondent

Let C.D. Ltd of (*address*) attend before the Judge on:

Date ....

Time ....

Place ....

On the hearing of an application by A.B. Ltd., the Applicant, for an order in the following terms:

1. That the Respondent may be restrained, whether by itself, himself, or by its, or his, servants or agents or otherwise howsoever, from presenting any petition to this Court, or any Court, for the winding-up of the above-named A.B. Ltd. ("the Company") based on the sum of £.......................claimed in the statutory demand dated the .... day of ....20....... served on the Company on .... 20.....

2. Or that such other order may be made as to the Court shall seem fit.

3. That the costs of this application may be paid by the Respondent to the Applicant.

The grounds upon which the Applicant claims to be entitled to the relief sought herein are set out in the witness statement of G.H. made on .... 20....... and filed herein, a true copy of which is served herewith.

It is intended to serve this application on C.D. Ltd. whose registered office is situated at:

(*address*)..

Or:

It is not intended to serve any person with this application.

The Applicant's address for service is: ....
....
....

DATED .... 20....   SIGNATURE ....

Applicant

If you do not attend, the court may make such order as it thinks fit.

(*Copied by kind permission of Butterworths-Tolley*)

APPLICATION for order to restrain advertisement of winding-up petition

Either, *in the High Court:*

IN THE HIGH COURT OF JUSTICE   No........ of ....20 ......

Chancery Division
[Companies Court]
[............ District Registry]

Or, *in the county court:*

IN THE .... COUNTY COURT   No........ of ....20 ......

Then, *in any case:*

In the Matter of A.B. Ltd
And in the Matter of the Insolvency Act 1986

Between A.B. Ltd   Applicant

                              and

          C.D. Ltd   Respondent

Take Notice that A.B. Ltd. intends to apply to the Judge on:

Date ....

Time ....

Place ....

For an order in the following terms:

(1)   that C.D. the Petitioner named in the petition presented to this
        Court on .... 20....... for the winding-up of the Ap-
        plicant Company, be restrained from proceeding further upon
        the Petition whether by advertising the same or otherwise;

(2)   that the Petition be removed from the file of proceedings; and

(3)   that the Petitioner do pay the costs of this application.

        The grounds upon which the Applicant Company claims to be
        entitled to the relief sought herein are set out in the witness
        statement of G.H., made on (*insert date*) ....

20......... and filed herein, a true copy of which is served herewith.

The address for service of the Applicant Company is: ....
....

DATED .... 20....   SIGNATURE ....
                                                                 Applicant

If you do not attend, the court may make such order as it thinks fit.

(Copied by kind permission of Butterworths-Tolley)

Specimen Witness Statement in support of application for order either restraining presentation of a petition, or restraining the advertisement of a petition and that the petition be struck out.

Applicant: G.H. (*insert surname*): 1ˢᵗ: G.H.1, ...20...........

Either, *in the High Court:*

> IN THE HIGH COURT OF JUSTICE   No........ of ....20 ......
> Chancery Division
>   [Companies Court]
>   [........... District Registry]

Or, *in the county court:*

IN THE .... COUNTY COURT   No........ of ....20 ......

Then, *in any case:*

In the Matter of A.B. Ltd

And in the Matter of the Insolvency Act 1986

Between	A.B. Ltd	Applicant
	and	
	C.D. Ltd	Respondent

I, G.H. (*state full name of witness*), of (*state residence or workplace and the position held*), state as follows:

1.   I am the (*position held*) in the Applicant Company, by which I am duly authorised to make this witness statement. Where the matters stated are within my own knowledge they are true, all other matters are to the best of my knowledge and belief true and I have explained the source of information on which my belief is based.

2.   On..... .... 20........, the Respondent C. D. Ltd. of (*address*) by their Solicitors E. F. & Co., (*address*) served on the Applicant Company at the address of its registered office a demand in the prescribed form for payment of £........., a copy of which is marked "G.H.1", and exhibited hereto. It is stated in the demand that the consideration for the debt is (*state what the debt is for*).

Where petition is sought to be restrained

3.   On ....20......., the Respondent C.D. Ltd. served on
        the Applicant Company a petition for the winding-up of the
        Applicant Company, which it had presented at this court
        on .... 20........

4.   The goods were defective and unsaleable.

5.   There have been telephone conversations and correspondence
        with Solicitors for C.D. Ltd. giving full particulars of the
        above matters and warning of the consequences of proceeding
        further with the statutory demand [by presenting a petition
        to wind up] or [by advertising the said petition], including a
        warning that the Applicant Company would apply for an in-
        junction. I refer to such correspondence in a bundle marked
        "G.H.2", and exhibited hereto.

6.   In the circumstances, I ask that the Respondent C.D. Ltd. be
        restrained [from presenting to this or any other court a peti-
        tion for the winding-up of the Applicant Company based on
        the said alleged debt and on non-compliance with the said
        demand]

        Or,

        [from proceeding with the said petition by advertising or oth-
        erwise, and that the said petition be struck out with costs].

        (Delete whichever clause is not appropriate).

STATEMENT OF TRUTH

This witness statement was made and signed at *(address)* on *(date)* by
me, *(state name)*.

I believe that the facts stated in this witness statement are true............
                                                    Signature of witness
.....................................*(print full name clearly)*

(Copied by kind permission of Butterworths-Tolley)

PART 2

Schedule 4A to the Insolvency Act 1986 (as amended)

BANKRUPTCY RESTRICTIONS ORDER AND UNDERTAKING

1.   **Bankruptcy restrictions order**

1(1) A bankruptcy restrictions order may be made by the court.

1(2) An order may be made only on the application of:

(a) the Secretary of State, or

(b) the official receiver acting on a direction of the Secretary of State.

2.   **Grounds for making the order**

2(1) The court shall grant an application for a bankruptcy restrictions order if it thinks it appropriate having regard to the conduct of the bankrupt (whether before or after the making of the bankruptcy order).

2(2) The court shall, in particular, take into account any of the following kinds of behaviour on the part of the bankrupt:

(a) failing to keep records which account for a loss of property by the bankrupt, or by a business carried on by him, where the loss occurred in the period beginning 2 years before petition and ending with the date of the application;

(b) failing to produce records of that kind on demand by the official receiver or the trustee;

(c) entering into a transaction at an undervalue;

(d) giving a preference;

(e) making an excessive pension contribution;

(f) a failure to supply goods or services which were wholly or partly paid for which gave rise to a claim provable in the bankruptcy

(g) trading at a time before commencement of the bankruptcy when the bankrupt knew or ought to have known that he was himself unable to pay his debts;

(h) incurring, before commencement of the bankruptcy, a debt which the bankrupt had no reasonable expectation of being able to pay;

(i) failing to account satisfactorily to the court, the official receiver or the trustee for a loss of property or for an insufficiency of property to meet bankruptcy debts;

(j) carrying on any gambling, rash and hazardous speculation or unreasonable extravagance which may have materially contributed to or increased the extent of the bankruptcy or which took place between presentation of the petition and commencement of the bankruptcy;

(k) neglect of business affairs of a kind which may have materially contributed to or increased the extent of the bankruptcy;

(l) fraud or fraudulent breach of trust;

(m) failing to co-operate with the official receiver or the trustee.

2(3) The court shall also, in particular, consider whether the bankrupt was an undischarged bankrupt at some time during the period of six years ending with the date of the bankruptcy to which the application relates.

PART 3

Addresses of bodies and organisations offering legal aid and assistance

The Courts Service (advice on courts)
Website: *www.hmcourts-service.gov.uk*

The Insolvency Service
Website: *www.insolvency.gov.uk*
Website: *www.bankruptcyadviceservice.co.uk*

Insolvency helpline: *www.insolvencyhelpline.co.uk*
Debts programme: *www.insolvency/gov.uk/information*

The Legal Services Commission
Website: *www.legalservices.gov.uk*
Tel (Head Office):   020 7759 0000

There are also regional offices : a list is in Part 4.

Law Centres (the Law Centres Federation)
Website: *www.lawcentres.org.uk*
e-mail: *info@lawcentres.org.uk*

A list of Law Centres is in Part 4, below.

Royal Courts of Justice Advice Bureau

At the Royal Courts of Justice, in the Strand in London, there is an Advice Bureau which is free, independent and confidential, to people who do not have a lawyer to represent them.

The Bureau maintains a "Bankruptcy Court Advice Desk", which gives free legal advice to people facing bankruptcy petitions in the High Court, or wishing to present their own petitions to make themselves bankrupt, or who have already been made bankrupt.

They can obtain advice on setting aside Statutory Demands (see Part II, above), on negotiating settlements with their creditors to avoid bankruptcy, and on obtaining adjournments of court proceedings to enable them to seek further advice or assistance, including the provision of free representation. People wishing to present their own bankruptcy petitions (see Chapter 6 above) can receive advice about the effects of going bankrupt, and can have their Debtor's Petition forms checked, or (by appointment) can be helped to complete their Debtor's Petition forms.

People who are already bankrupt can get advice about Income Payment Orders or Agreements (see Chapter 19, above), about Bankruptcy Restriction Orders or Undertakings (see Chapter 22 above) and about annulment of the bankruptcy order (see Chapter 23, above).

This Advice Desk is situated in the Thomas More Building. The Desk may also, in cases which involve difficult legal problems or complicated facts, be able to introduce the litigant to a new pilot scheme, "The Personal Insolvency Litigation and Advice Scheme" ("PILARS").

The PILARS service aims to provide clients without a lawyer, who are nominated by the Advice Desk, with a barrister to appear in court without fee, to fight their case. The barristers, who are volunteers and work for free, are draw from commercial barrister's chambers. PILARS does not deal directly with the public, but only through the Advice Desk.

The website address of the Advice Desk is www.rcjadvice.org.uk where information can be obtained on appointment times and contact details. Its telephone number is 0207 947 6000.

Citizens Advice
Website: *www.citizensadvice.org.uk*   (can provide details of all Citizens Advice Bureaux).

Bar ProBono Unit

Website: *www.barprono.org.uk*

Solicitors ProBono Group (operating under the name "LawWorks")

Website: *www.lawworks.org.uk*
e-mail: *enquiries@lawworks.org.uk*

The Bankruptcy Advisory Service (at Hull)

e-mail: *gill@bankruptcyadvisoryservice.co.uk*
Tel: 01482 633034 / 5

PART 4

List of regional offices of Legal Services Commission

Head Office
85 Gray's Inn Road
London WC1X 8TX
Tel: 020 7759 0000

Chester Office
2nd Floor, Pepper House
Pepper Row
Chester CH1 1DW
Tel: 01244 404500

East Midlands Office
Regional Office
1st Floor, Fothergill House
16 King Street
Nottingham NG1 2AS
Tel: 0115 908 4200

Eastern Regional Office
62-68 Hills Road
Cambridge CB2 1LA
Tel: 01223 417800

London Regional Office
29-37 Red Lion Street
London WC1R 4PP
Tel: 020 7759 1500

Merseyside Regional Office
2nd Floor, Cavern Court
8 Mathew Street
Liverpool L2 6RE
Tel: 0151 242 5200

North East Regional Office
Eagle Star House
Fenkle Street
Newcastle-upon-Tyne NE1 5RU
Tel: 0191 244 5800

North Western Regional Office
2nd Floor, Lee House
90 Great Bridgewater Street
Manchester M1 5JW
Tel: 0161 244 5000

South East Regional Office
Reading
80 King's Road
Reading RG1 4LT
Tel: 01189 558600

Brighton
3rd/4th Floor, Invicta House
Trafalgar Place, Cheapside
Brighton BN1 4FR
Tel: 01273 878800

South Western Regional Office
33-35 Queen Square
Bristol BS1 4LU
Tel: 0117 302 3000

Wales Office
Marland House
Central Square
Cardiff CF10 1PF
Tel: 02920 647100

West Midlands Regional Office
Centre City Podium
5 Hill Street
Birmingham B5 4UD
Tel: 0121 665 4700

Yorkshire and Humberside Regional Office
Harcourt House
Chancellor Court
21 The Calls
Leeds LS2 7EH
Tel: 0113 390 7300

Website address:
www.legalservices.gov.uk

PART 5

List of Law Centres : November 2006

Avon and Bristol Law Centre
2 Moon Street
Bristol BS2 8QE
Tel: 0117 924 8662
Fax: 0117 924 8020
e-mail: mail@ablc.demon.co.uk

Barnet Law Service (Law Centre)
9 Bell Lane
London NW4 2BP
Tel: 020 8203 4141
Fax: 020 8203 8042
e-mail: bcls@barnetlaw.co.uk

Battersea Law Centre (SWLLC)
14 York Road
London SW11 3QA
Tel: 020 7585 0716
Fax: 020 7585 0718
e-mail:
solicitors@battersealawcentre.fsnet.co.uk

Belfast Law Centre
See: Law Centre (Northern Ireland)

Bradford Law Centre
31 Manor Row
Bradford BD1 4PX
Tel: 01274 306 617
Fax: 01274 390 939
e-mail: enquiries@bradfordlawcentre.co.uk

Brent Community Law Centre
389 High Road
Willesden
London NW10 2JR
Tel: 020 8451 1122
Fax: 020 8830 2462
e-mail: brentlaw@brentlaw.org.uk

Bury Law Centre
8 Bank Street
Bury BL9 0DL
Tel: 0161 272 0666
Fax: 0161 272 0031
e-mail: info@burylawcentre.co.uk

Cambridge House Law Centre
137 Camberwell Road
London SE5 0HF
Tel: 020 7703 3051/ 020 7701 9499
Fax: 020 7277 0401
e-mail:
lawcentre@cambridgehouseandtalbot.org.uk

Camden Community Law Centre
2 Prince of Wales Road
London NW5 3LQ
Tel: 020 7284 6510
Fax: 020 7267 6218
e-mail: admin@cclc.org.uk

Cardiff Law Centre
41/42 Clifton Street
Cardiff CF24 1LS
Tel: 029 20498 117
Fax: 029 20497 118
e-mail: cardiff.lawcentre@dial.pipex.com

Carlisle Law Centre
8 Spencer Street
Carlisle CA1 1BG
Tel: 01228 515 129
Fax: 01228 515 819
e-mail: information@communitylaw.org.uk

Central London Law Centre
19 Whitcomb Street
London WC2H 7HA
Tel: 020 7839 2998
Fax: 020 7839 6158

Chesterfield Law Centre
44 Park Road
Chesterfield S40 1XZ
Tel: 01246 550 674
Fax: 01246 551 069
e-mail: clc@chesterfieldlawcentre.org.uk

Coventry Law Centre
The Bridge
Broadgate
Coventry, CV1 1NG
Tel: 024 7622 3053
Fax: 024 7622 8551
e-mail: enquiries@covlaw.org.uk

Croydon & Sutton Law Centre (SWLLC)
79 Park Lane
Croydon CF0 1JG
Tel: 020 8667 9226
Fax: 020 8662 8079

Derby Law Centre
PO Box 173
The Market Hall
Derby DE1 9XN
Tel: 01332 344 557
Fax: 01332 614 755
e-mail: DerbyLaw@dial.pipex.com

Devon Law Centre
2nd Floor, Fox House
8-10 Whimple Street
Plymouth
Devon PL1 2DH
Tel: 01752 519 794
Fax: 01752 519 795
e-mail: information@devonlawcentre.org.uk

Enfield Law Centre
38 Market Square (1st Floor)
Edmonton Green
Edmonton B9 0TZ
Tel: 020 807 8888
Fax: 020 807 8844
e-mail: info@enfieldlawcentre.org.uk

Gateshead Law Centre
1 Walker Terrace
Gateshead NE8 1EB
Tel: 0191 440 8585
Tel. advice M-F: 0191 440 8575
Fax: 0191 449 8580
e-mail: info@glclaw.org

Gloucester Law Centre
75-81 Eastgate Street
Gloucester GL1 1PN
Tel: 01452 423 492
Fax: 01452 387 594
e-mail: admin@gloucesterlawcentre.co.uk

Greenwich Community Law Centre
187 Trafalgar Road
London SE10 9EQ
Tel: 020 8305 3350
Fax: 020 8858 5253
e-mail: info@gclc.co.uk

Hackney Community Law Centre
8 Lower Clapton Road
London E5 0PD
Tel: 020 8985 8364
Fax: 020 8533 2018
e-mail: info@hclc.org.uk

Hammersmith & Fulham Law Centre
142/144 King Street
London W6 0QU
Tel: 020 8741 4021
Fax: 020 8741 1450
e-mail: hflaw@hflaw.org.uk

Harehills & Chapeltown Law Centre
263 Roundhay Road
Leeds LS8 4HS
Tel: 0113 249 1100
Fax: 0113 235 1185
e-mail: admin@leedslawcentre.org.uk

Haringey Law Centre
754-758 High Road
Tottenham
London N17 0AL
Tel: 020 8808 5354
Fax: 020 8801 1516
e-mail: tottenhamlawcentre@tiscali.co.uk

Hillingdon Law Centre
12 Harold Avenue
Hayes,
Middlesex UB3 4QW
Tel: 020 8561 9400
Fax: 020 8756 0837
e-mail: hillingdon@lawyersonline.co.uk

Hounslow Law Centre
51 Lampton Road
Hounslow
Middlesex TW3 1LY
Tel: 020 8570 9505
Fax: 020 8572 0730
e-mail: hounslowc@dial.pipex.com

Isle of Wight Law Centre
Exchange House
St Cross Lane
Newport, Isle of Wight PO30 5BZ
Tel: 01983 524715
Fax: 01983 522606
e-mail: iowlc@iowlc.org.uk

Islington Law Centre
161 Hornsey Road
London N7 6DU
Tel: 020 7607 2461
Fax: 020 7700 0072
e-mail: info@islingtonlaw.org.uk

**Kingston & Richmond Law Centre
(SWLLC)**
Siddeley House
50 Canbury Park Road
Kingston, Surrey
KT2 6LX
Tel: 020 8547 2882
Fax: 020 8547 2350

Kirklees Law Centre
Units 11/12, Empire House
Wakefield Old Road
Dewsbury
West Yorkshire WF12 8DJ
Tel: 01924 439829
Fax: 01924 868140

Lambeth Law Centre
Unit 47, Eurolink Business Centre
40 Effra Road
London SW2 1BZ
Tel: 020 7737 9781
Fax: 020 7274 7386
e-mail: Admin@lambethlawcentre.org.
London Race Discrimination Unit
Advice Line: 020 7737 9780

Law Centre (Northern Ireland)
124 Donegall Street
Belfast BT1 2GY
Tel: 028 9024 4401
Textphone: 028 9023 9938
Fax: 028 9023 6340
e-mail: admin.belfast@lawcentreni.org

**Law Centre (Northern Ireland)
Western Area**
9 Clarendon Street
Derry BT48 7EP
Tel: 028 7126 2433
Fax: 028 7126 2343
e-mail: admin.derry@lawcentreniwest.org

Leicester Law Centre
20 Millstone Lane
Leicester LE1 5JN
Tel: 0116 242 1160
Fax: 0116 255 6431
e-mail: info@leicesterlawcentre.co.uk

Lewisham Law Centre
28 Deptford High Street
London SE8 4AF
Tel: 020 8692 5355
Fax: 020 8694 2516
e-mail: info@lewishamlawcentre.org.uk

Liverpool 8 Law Centre
34/36 Princes Road
Liverpool
L8 1TH
Tel: 0151 709 7222
Fax: 0151 708 8178
e-mail: l8law@liverpool8lawcentre.co.uk

Luton Law Centre
6th Floor, Cresta House
Alma Street
Luton LU1 2PL
Tel: 01582 481 000
Fax: 01582 482 581

Newcastle Law Centre
1st Floor
1 Charlotte Square
Newcastle-upon-Tyne
NE1 4XF
Tel: 0191 230 4777
Fax: 0191 233 0295
e-mail: info@newcastlelawcentre.co.uk

North Kensington Law Centre
74 Golborne Road
London W10 5PS
Tel: 020 8969 7473
Fax: 020 8968 0934
e-mail: info@nklc.co.uk

North Manchester Law Centre
Harpurhey District Centre
Off Rochdale Road
Harpurhey
Manchester M9 4DH
Tel: 0161 205 5040
Fax: 0161 205 8654
e-mail: info@nmlc.org.uk

Nottingham Law Centre
119 Radford Road
Nottingham NG7 5DU
Tel: 0115 978 7813
Fax: 0115 979 2969
e-mail: nottlawcentre@btconnect.com

Oldham Law Centre
1st Floor, Archway House
Bridge Street
Oldham OL1 1ED
Tel: 0161 627 0925
Fax: 0161 620 3411
e-mail: admin@oldhamlawcentre.org

Paddington Law Centre
439 Harrow Road
London W10 4RE
Tel: 020 8960 3155
Fax: 020 8968 0417
e-mail: paddinglaw@btconnect.com

Plumstead Community Law Centre
105 Plumstead High Street
London SE18 1SB
Tel: 020 8855 9817
Fax: 020 8316 7903
e-mail: pclc@dial.pipex.com

Rochdale Law Centre
15 Drake Street
Rochdale OL16 4RE
Tel: 01706 657 766
Fax: 01706 346 558
e-mail: info@rochdalelawcentre.org.uk
www.rochdalelawcentre.org.uk

Rotherham Law Centre
88 Wellgate
Rotherham
S60 2LP
Tel: 01709 838 988
e-mail: rotherhamlawcentre@btconnect.com

Saltley & Nechells Law Centre
2 Alum Rock Road
Saltley
Birmingham B8 1JB
Tel: 0121 328 2307
Fax: 0121 327 7486
e-mail: snlc@btconnect.com

Sheffield Law Centre
1st Floor, Waverley House
10 Joiner Street
Sheffield S3 8GW
Tel: 0114 273 1501
Fax: 0114 273 1501
e-mail: post@slc.org.uk

South Manchester Law Centre
584 Stockport Road
Manchester M13 0RQ
Tel: 0161 225 5111
Fax: 0161 224 0210
e-mail: admin@smlc.org.uk

Southwark Law Centre
Hanover Park House
14-16 Hanover Park
Peckham, London SE15 5HG
Tel: 010 7732 2008
Fax: 020 7732 2034
e-mail: general@southwarklawcentre.org.uk

Springfield Law Centre
Springfield Hospital
Glenburnie Road
London SW17 7DJ
Tel: 020 8767 6884
Fax: 020 8767 6996
e-mail:
thelawcentre@springfieldhospital.freeserve.co.uk

Stockport Law Centre
85 Wellington Road South
Stockport
SK1 3SL
Tel: 0161 476 6336
Fax: 0161 476 2719

Streetwise Community Law Centre
1-3 Anerley Station Road
Penge
London SE20 8PY
Tel: 020 8778 5854
Fax: 020 8776 9392
(Young people up to 25 only)

Surrey Law Centre
Room 1, Unit 15A
Monument Way Depot
Woking, GU21 5LY
Tel: 01483 214 000
Fax: 01483 750 770
e-mail: info@surreylawcentre.org

Thamesmead Law Centre
*(Attached to Plumstead Community Law
Centre)*
St Paul's Churchyard
Bentham Road
London SE28 8AS
Tel: 020 8311 0555
Fax: 020 8320 5655

Tower Hamlets Law Centre
214 Whitechapel Road
London E1 1BJ
Tel: 020 7247 8998
Fax: 020 7247 9424

Trafford Law Centre
4th Floor, John Darby House
88-92 Talbot Road
Old Trafford
Manchester M16 0GS
Tel: 0161 872 3669
Fax: 0161 872 2208
e-mail: admin@traffordlawcentre.org.uk

Vauxhall Law and Information Centre
Vauxhall Training and Enterprise Centre
Silvester Street
Liverpool L5 8SE
Tel: 0151 482 2001
Fax: 0151 207 4948

**Wandsworth & Merton Law Centre
(SWLLC)**
101a Tooting High Street
London SW17 0SU
Tel: 020 8767 2777
Fax: 020 8767 2711

**Wandsworth & Merton Law Centre (Merton)
(SWLLC)**
South London Tamil Welfare Office
36 High Street
Colliers Wood
London SW19
Tel: 020 8543 4069
Fax: 020 8542 3289

Wiltshire Law Centre
Temple House
115-188 Commercial Road
Swindon SN1 5PL
Tel: 01793 486 926 (Voice and Minicomb)
Fax: 01793 432 193
e-mail: wiltslawcentre@dial.pipex.com

Wythenshawe Law Centre
260 Brownley Road
Wythenshawe
Manchester M22 5EB
Tel: 0161 498 0905/6
Fax: 0161 498 0750
e-mail: info@wlawcentre.co.uk

LCF Associate Members

AIRE
Advice on Individual Rights in Europe
Third Floor
17 Red Lion Square
London WC1R 4QH
Tel: 020 7831 3850
Fax: 020 7404 7760
e-mail: aire@btinternet.com
*(Note: AIRE do not give advice directly to
the public)*

Castlemilk Law and Money Advice Centre
30-32 Dougrie Drive
Castlemilk
Glasgow G45 9AD
Tel: 0141 634 0313
Fax: 0141 634 1944
e-mail:
castlemilk@lawcentrel.freeserve.co.uk

The Disability Law Service
Ground Floor
30-45 Cavell Street
London E1 2BP
Tel: 020 7791 9800
Minicom: 020 7791 9801
Fax: 020 7791 9802
e-mail: advice@dls.org.uk
website: www.dls.org.uk

EarthRights
Little Orchard
School Lane
Mole Hill Green
Takeley,
Essex CM22 6PJ
Tel: 01279 870391
e-mail: john@earthrights.org.uk

Free Legal Advice Centre (Ireland)
13 Lower Dorset Street
Dublin 1
Ireland
Tel: 00353 1 874 5690
Fax: 00353 1 874 5320
e-mail: info@flac.i.e.
website: www.flac.ie

Greater Manchester Immigration Aid Unit
1 Delaunays Road
Crumpsall Green
Manchester, M8 4QS
Tel: 0161 740 7722
Fax: 0161 740 5172
e-mail: gmiau@ein.org.uk

Mary Ward Legal Centre
26-27 Boswell Street
London WC1N 3JZ
Tel: 020 7831 7079
Fax: 020 7831 5431
e-mail: enquiries@marywardlegal.org.uk
website: www.marywadlegal.org.uk

For Law Centres based in Scotland, please contact:

Scottish Association of Law Centres
C/o Govan Law Centre
47 Burleigh Street
Govan
Glasgow G15 8TE
Tel: 0141 440 2503
Fax: 0141 445 3934
Website: www.govanlc.com

INDEX

More Practical Handbooks from XPL...

Small Claims Procedure: A Practical Guide
HHJ Pearl
The best book for lay or professional readers – highly practical yet authoritative.

Welfare Benefits and Tax Credits: Annual Volume
Keith Puttick
Issued annually, this one volume guide provides all required to assess entitlement, rates and appeals procedures

www.xplpublishing.com

Printed in the United Kingdom
by Lightning Source UK Ltd.
118544UK00001B/172-189